D1104774

IRAN UNDER KHATAMI

A Political, Economic, and Military Assessment

• • •

Patrick Clawson
Michael Eisenstadt
Eliyahu Kanovsky
David Menashri

• • •

A Washington Institute Monograph

• • •

THE WASHINGTON INSTITUTE FOR NEAR EAST POLICY

© 1998 by the Washington Institute for Near East Policy

Published in 1998 in the United States of America by the Washington Institute for Near East Policy, 1828 L Street NW, Suite 1050, Washington, DC 20036.

Library of Congress Cataloging-in-Publication Data

Iran under Khatami : a political, economic, and military assessment / Patrick L. Clawson ... [et al.].
      p.   cm.
   ISBN 0-944029-27-2 (pbk.)
    1. Iran—Politics and government—1997–   2. Khatami, Muhammad. 3. Iran—Economic conditions—1997–   4. Iran—Foreign relations—1997–   5. Iran—Military policy.
I. Clawson, Patrick, 1951– .
DS318.9.I73   1998
955.05'43—dc21   98-39718
                                             CIP

Cover design by Monica Neal Hertzman. Cover image AFP Photo/ Jamshid Bairami/Corbis.

CONTENTS

Contributors

Patrick Clawson is director for research at The Washington Institute for Near East Policy and senior editor of the *Middle East Quarterly*. Previously, he was a senior research professor at the Institute for National Strategic Studies of the National Defense University and editor of INSS's flagship annual publication, *Strategic Assessment.*

Michael Eisenstadt is a senior fellow at The Washington Institute. He is the coauthor most recently of two Washington Institute monographs, *'Knives, Tanks, and Missiles': Israel's Security Revolution* and *Iraq Strategy Review: Options for U.S. Policy* (Washington Institute, 1998). He previously served as an analyst with the U.S. Army and as a researcher for the U.S. Air Force *Gulf War Air Power Survey (GWAPS).*

Eliyahu Kanovsky is professor of economics and a senior research associate at the BESA Center for Strategic Studies at Bar Ilan University in Israel, and is also the Ludwig Jesselson Visiting Professor of Economics at Yeshiva University in New York. He is the author of numerous studies of the economics of the Middle East, including five previous Washington Institute Policy Papers.

David Menashri is a senior research fellow at Tel Aviv University's Moshe Dayan Center for Middle Eastern and African Studies and chair of the university's Department of Middle Eastern and African History. The author and editor of several books on Iran, he also spent two years conducting field research in the country in the late 1970s on the eve of the Islamic revolution.

• • •

PREFACE

Iranian president Muhammad Khatami has generated much interest since taking office in August 1997. On the surface, he seems quite different from the Islamic Republic's earlier leaders: He talks about dialogue of civilizations, not about death to America, the Great Satan. But at the same time, under his leadership, Iran has test-fired its first missile with a range that includes much of the Middle East, has maintained its unrelenting hostility toward Israel, and has affirmed its position as the region's leading supporter of terrorism.

The chapters that follow explore the contradictions in Khatami's Iran as well as their implications for U.S. policy. They build upon three earlier Policy Papers issued in 1996–1997: one by David Menashri on Iranian domestic politics, another by Eliyahu Kanovsky on the economy, and a third by Michael Eisenstadt on the military.

In the arena of foreign policy, Khatami has enjoyed his greatest successes. The Europeans and even the United States are searching for an improvement in relations. At a time when the Arab–Israeli peace process is doing poorly, the coalition containing Iraqi president Saddam Husayn is crumbling, and South Asia's nuclear weapons are major challenges, Iran looks to many in Washington like one country in the region where the U.S. government could achieve a diplomatic "breakthrough."

In their updates for this volume, Menashri and Kanovsky show that things are not going so well for Khatami at home. The economy has been hit hard by declining oil prices, compounded by the government's inaction on fixing structural problems. On the political scene, despite Khatami's continuing strong popularity, his conservative opponents have regained their footing and are vigorously competing with him for control over the levers of power. By contrast, as Eisenstadt explains, since Khatami's election, Iran has made real and troubling strides on the military front in promoting the indigenous production of modern weapons, including missiles.

Unfortunately, as Eisenstadt and Patrick Clawson explain, the reality of Khatami's actual influence on policymaking and the prospects for real improvement in U.S.–Iranian relations are not hopeful. Aside from the relatively moderate tone of some official rhetoric, little of substance has changed in the three key areas of concern: support for terrorism, pursuit of weapons of mass destruction, and undermining the peace process. Nevertheless, there is much the U.S. government can do to exploit popular disillusionment within the Islamic Republic—exemplified by the 70 percent of the electorate that voted for the regime's least preferred candidate—while maintaining firm pressure on Tehran to change its unacceptable behavior.

At a time of ferment and change in Iran, the U.S. government needs to consider how to adapt its policies to changing perceptions of Iran, while at the same time holding firm on America's unswerving goals. We hope that *Iran Under Khatami* will contribute to a better understanding of how Iran is evolving and how U.S. policy can respond with creativity and ingenuity.

Mike Stein
President

Barbi Weinberg
Chairman

Chapter 1

THE KHATAMI PARADOX

Patrick Clawson

Muhammad Khatami's surprise victory in the May 23, 1997, Iranian presidential election generated much enthusiasm at home and much interest abroad. For Iranians, the massive popular mandate—Khatami received 70 percent of the vote with a nearly 90 percent turnout—showed their disillusionment with the ruling establishment. Khatami's victory stirred hopes that change was possible within the current system, hopes reinforced by Khatami's symbolic gestures showing a new leadership style (riding Tehran buses, dispensing with large entourages, and mixing with common people). Abroad—in the Arab world, in Europe, and even in the United States—the new leadership was seen as an opportunity to break with the rigidity of the past and to put relations on a new, nonhostile footing. In Washington, President Bill Clinton's hope was that Khatami's election would "bode well for the future." The essays that follow examine how that hope has held up since Khatami took office in August 1997.

The analysis here is an update of three 1996–1997 publications from The Washington Institute: Michael Eisenstadt's *Iranian Military Power: Capabilities and Intentions* (Policy Paper no. 42), David Menashri's *Revolution at a Crossroads: Iran's Domestic Politics and Regional Ambitions* (Policy Paper no. 43), and Eliyahu Kanovsky's *Iran's Economic Morass: Mismanagement and Decline under the Islamic Republic* (Policy Paper no. 44). Because those publications cover in detail developments through 1996, the analysis here is only of developments since 1997.

The theme of this volume is paradox: Khatami campaigned

1

on domestic issues while saying little on foreign and security policy, but his first year in office saw progress on the latter front while domestic policy has been a continuing struggle. The forecast offered here is that, going into his second year, Khatami faces more of the same. The domestic scene is mixed at best: The economy has been hit hard by declining oil prices, and Khatami's conservative opponents have proved politically resilient. By contrast, foreign policy is going well, with even the United States searching for an improvement in relations, and on the security front, Iran has made real—and troubling— strides in promoting the indigenous production of modern weapons, including missiles.

PROBLEMS AT HOME

As Menashri explains, Khatami went from strength to strength on the domestic political scene in his first few months. The Majlis (parliament) approved his entire cabinet, as his conservative opponents seemed shell-shocked and unsure how to react. Yet, the situation changed by the spring of 1998.

An unusual problem emerged for Khatami in that a numbers of his supporters were dissatisfied with the slow pace of change and the harsh realities of Islamist rule. These people rallied around Ayatollah Hosein 'Ali Montazeri, for example, mounting major demonstrations in early March, early April, and mid-May. In turn, these demonstrations angered the hardline conservatives who felt the administration was not doing enough to maintain public order.

Thus, the conservative opposition went on the attack using two key institutions it controls, the Majlis and the judiciary. Tehran mayor Gholam-Hosein Karbaschi was arrested on April 5 on transparently political charges of corruption; Karbaschi had been well known for raising funds through dubiously legal means, but he used the money mostly to improve municipal services, unlike the many officials who steal openly for their own benefit. Then, after months of criticizing Interior Minister 'Abdollah Nuri for allowing students to protest against conservative repression (and in support of Montazeri) and for licensing free-minded publications, the Majlis dismissed him on June 21. In Karbaschi's case, despite massive street protests that forced his release pending a judicial verdict, he was subsequently tried and found guilty on July 23. In sum, Khatami's conservative opponents seem to have regained their nerve, and they hold many levers of power.

If the political scene is fraught with danger for reformers, the economic outlook is even more gloomy. Kanovksy documents the fundamental structural economic problems facing Islamic Iran. The country's reliance on oil and gas has deepened since the time of the shah, such that the Iranian government relies on these two exports for most of its revenue and 80 percent of the country's foreign exchange. Yet, the oil and gas industry itself has atrophied; only massive foreign capital can renew it. Attracting that capital would not be easy even if there were no political risk concerns: The world is awash in cheap oil, and many countries are vying to win investments by the oil and gas multinationals. As for Iran's non-oil economy, the Khatami coalition is deeply torn between those who want to unleash market forces and those who yearn for a return to the early revolutionary practices of strict controls in the name of social justice. Kanovsky explains that even in those areas where Khatami has promised reform, little has been done and no coherent program for progress has been proposed. Given the gloomy oil prices of 1998, Khatami will be lucky if the economy does not slide back into the massive deficit financing of the early 1990s, which would run the risk of both repeating the foreign debt crisis if too much is borrowed abroad and reigniting high inflation if too much money is printed to cover the budget deficits.

SUCCESS AT IMPROVING NATIONAL SECURITY

Whereas the domestic scene has been difficult for Khatami, foreign affairs for him have been one triumph after another. The December 1997 Organization of the Islamic Conference (OIC) summit in Tehran went well both for Iran and for Khatami personally. In the following months, relations with Iran's Gulf neighbors improved remarkably, with frequent ministerial visits. Saudi Arabia did little to investigate a possible Iranian role in the June 1996 Khobar Towers bombing that killed 19 Americans, evidently out of a desire to avoid finding evidence of Iranian involvement. Meanwhile, Iranian–European relations warmed with the resumption of high-level visits and regular meetings—rebaptized as constructive engagement rather than critical dialogue, to avoid the implication that Europe was critical of Iranian behavior. The April 1997 German court verdict in the bombing of Berlin's Mykonos disco, which held Iran's leadership personally responsible for terror assassinations on European soil, was forgotten. Europe's preoccupation became how to support Khatami, who was seen as the great liberal hope.

Perhaps Khatami's most dramatic initiative was on Iranian–American relations. His January 7, 1998, interview with CNN caught the American imagination, even though his softer rhetoric often masked unchanged positions. For instance, many were satisfied with his comment about the 1979 U.S. embassy hostage crisis, which expressed regret for hurt feelings ("I do know that the feelings of the great American people have been hurt, and of course I regret it"), but not for the egregious violation of international law that the seizure of the embassy represented. His hardline remarks ("certain foreign policy decisions of the U.S. are made in Tel Aviv and not in Washington") were passed over in the enthusiastic reception of his call for "civilizational dialogue." That call was followed soon by the first postrevolutionary visit to Iran by

American athletes, and it elevated to a higher profile the long-standing sport and scholarly contacts (for years, Iranians by the thousands—including Olympic teams and other athletes—have visited the United States). Khatami reiterated Iran's rejection of government-to-government dialogue, but the United States persisted, breathing life into its long-standing offer to hold such a dialogue. In a June 17, 1998, speech at the Asia Society in New York, Secretary of State Madeleine Albright welcomed "signs of change" in Iran, adding, "We are ready to explore further ways to build mutual confidence and avoid misunderstandings." In short, Khatami was able to create a perception of change that led to a less wary U.S. stance—and he did this without conceding on any of points of substance.

Khatami was also the beneficiary of a changed mood in the United States about economic sanctions, which had been the principal U.S. instrument to contain Iran. The changed mood had two causes. First and most important was European pressure. European opinion is unsympathetic to sanctions in general, on the theory that trade relations promote positive political change. Europeans were livid about the secondary boycott provisions of the Iran–Libya Sanctions Act (ILSA), which they regard as unacceptable in principle, irrespective of the purpose to which it is put. Faced with intense European hostility, in spring 1998 the United States clarified a change in policy that had been in the works since October 1997, namely, the retreat from the threat of a secondary boycott over European investment in Iranian oil and gas projects. This decision had little to do with developments in Iran, being based instead on the desire to avoid an open split in the Western alliance.

A secondary factor weakening support for Iran sanctions has been the U.S. business community's lobbying against sanctions as a whole, which is likely to intensify, as U.S. oil firms want the same freedom to invest in Iran that is now available to European firms. That lobbying has changed the mood in

Congress. Rather than considering broad sanctions, its 1997–1998 actions on Iran have been more focused. The Iran Missile-Proliferation Sanctions Act (IMPSA), which passed both houses overwhelmingly in June 1998, targeted only firms that were violating an international arms control agreement—in practice, certain Russian firms. Even so, President Clinton vetoed IMPSA, instead imposing by executive order sanctions on seven Russian firms that Moscow determined had violated Russian technology-export regulations. For Iran, the implication of the new sanctions-wary mood is that U.S. sanctions are not likely to become tougher and may in fact ease.

To be sure, not everything has been rosy for Iranian foreign policy during Khatami's first year. The fundamentalist Sunni Taliban in Afghanistan consolidated its hold on Kabul and advanced toward complete control over the entire country, despite Iranian supplies of arms and advisers to the Taliban's opponents. Taliban rule is a serious security problem for Iran, especially because more than a million Afghans work in Iran and the border is riddled with smuggling. Taliban members are viscerally hostile to Shi'a Islam and are politically allied with extremist Sunni terrorists active in Pakistan and eastern Iran, an area with a large Sunni minority.

Other than the Afghan setback, Khatami's first year was generally good for the Iranian military, because it made progress in addressing a major security shortcoming—namely, its dependence on potentially unreliable foreign arms-suppliers. Faced with this strategic vulnerability, Iran has for years wanted to manufacture its own weapons systems, but it rarely had much success. Despite years of effort, for instance, Iran made little progress toward an indigenous missile production capacity. This situation has changed recently, as demonstrated by the flight-test of the Shehab-3 missile, which has the range to reach Tel Aviv, Ankara, and Riyadh. That was not the only advance on the military industries front in Khatami's inaugural year. Iran also unveiled the Thunder-1 and -2 self-propelled guns, the *Tosan* (Fury) light tank, and the BMT-2 and Cobra armored personnel carriers; announced that production of the propeller-driven *Parastu* (Swallow) and jet-powered *Dorna* (Lark) training aircraft would commence shortly; and started mass production of the Boraq armored personnel carrier and the Zulfiqar main battle tank.

IMPLICATIONS FOR THE UNITED STATES

The debate about Iran policy in the United States has become a debate about whether to retain a hard line or to open up. Cast that way, the obvious winner has been to ease up, in response to the more open Iranian society that cheers visiting American wrestlers and witnesses vigorous political debate in a press remarkably free by regional standards. Indeed, U.S. policymakers have reason to be more excited about Iran than about anywhere else in the broad surrounding region. The Arab–Israeli peace process looks moribund, the coalition containing Iraqi president Saddam Husayn is crumbling, and South Asia's nuclear weapons are a massive headache. By contrast, with Iran, one can hope for a real breakthrough in relations, which would be both a major symbolic event and a true strategic victory—demonstrating that Western and Islamic civilizations need not be hostile, tempering fears about terrorism and proliferation to hostile powers, and improving the security of the unstable but vital Persian Gulf.

Unfortunately, the enthusiasm is out of place. A friendly embrace by the West—much less by the United States—could be dangerous for Khatami, as it might galvanize his conservative opponents and cast him as a puppet of the perfidious foreigners. Similarly, a friendly embrace is unwarranted given the lack of substantive—as compared with rhetorical—change in Iranian policy. Measured progress is the best that can be expected, even if Khatami decides that he wants reconciliation, given the domestic constraints he would face. Unlike Mao Tse-Tung's China, there is no common enemy that could bring Iran to cooperate with the United States, as long as Iran remains confident that Washington could and would prevent Saddam from exercising regional hegemony. Moreover, from a certain *realpolitik* perspective, Tehran's unwillingness to talk to Washington makes sense: The small gains could be offset by a major loss in influence among radical enemies of the West, who have given Iran an entree into arenas like the Balkans where it could never otherwise hope to be a player.

The most important consideration tempering any enthusiasm about reconciliation is that Iran under Khatami retains too many of the problematic policies of the past for the United States to rush into a friendly embrace. Khatami's frequent pronouncements on the evils of Zionism are no change from the past; his government continues to deliver arms to Hizballah. The government continues to assassinate dissidents abroad (though nearly all in northern Iraq). The development of missiles has been increased, as shown by the first test-flight of the Shehab-3 missile. And Iran has not fulfilled its reporting obligations under the Chemical Weapons Convention, which it joined in January 1998.

Nonetheless, Khatami's May 1997 election offers a number of opportunities for U.S. policy toward Iran. It holds out, for the first time since the 1979 revolution, the prospect of more normal relations with the Islamic Republic. But more important, it provides an opportunity for the United States to test the willingness of the new Iranian government to alter its policies in the areas of greatest concern to the United States: its active support of terrorism, its violent opposition to the Arab–Israeli peace process, and its continued pursuit of weapons of mass destruction (WMD) and the missiles to deliver them. The concluding chapter by Eisenstadt and Clawson analyzes the issues involved, with particular emphasis on how to evaluate the experience with sanctions and where next to take them.

The U.S. reaction to Khatami's election has been cautious, which is understandable in light of the history of the U.S.–Iran relationship. Washington, moreover, has been quite deft in responding to Iranian overtures, and the tone taken by senior U.S. policymakers can best be described as guardedly optimistic. Whereas the United States has taken a number of positive steps in responding to the new conditions in Tehran, more could and should be done—mainly in the realm of supporting people-to-people contacts.

Although such individual contacts can play an important role in reestablishing more normal relations between Iran and the United States, the major issues dividing the two countries will be resolved only in the context of government-to-government talks. Yet, Tehran has ruled out such contacts for now. Thus, substantive official contacts might still be years away. In the meantime, people-to-people contacts should continue, as they can help to create a psychological climate in both countries in which open, routine, official contacts can eventually occur, and the U.S. government should continue to support the Iranian people—the principle engine of political change in Tehran.

At the same time, Washington has been insufficiently resolute in maintaining the tough sanctions regime that has borne beneficial results in the past, and which is one of America's main bargaining chips vis-à-vis Iran. There is no contradiction in pursuing both dialogue and sanctions; the United States followed such a policy toward the Soviet Union for decades. At the same time, the United States should be prepared to ease or lift sanctions if Iran demonstrates that it has altered or abandoned the policies that led Washington to impose the sanctions in the first place. But it should not ease or lift the sanctions as an inducement to change those egregious policies.

Thus, Washington faces a challenge. It should continue its

efforts to establish an official dialogue with the regime in Tehran and to reach out to the Iranian people to support their desire for change. Yet, it needs to continue pressuring the regime, by applying economic sanctions, to change its policies on terrorism, the violent obstruction of the Arab–Israeli peace process, and WMD and missile development. Getting that mix right, and deciding on the proper policy tradeoffs with Tehran, will not be easy.

At the same time, barring major changes in Iranian foreign and defense policy, the United States should continue with efforts to delay and obstruct Iran's efforts to modernize and expand its armed forces—particularly in the WMD and missile arena. Delay buys time for the United States and its allies to develop countermeasures (like the U.S.-funded Israeli Arrow missile defense program). Plus, the longer required for the development of WMD and missiles, the likelier that during the meantime, less hostile elements will control Iranian foreign policy—meaning they may cancel the WMD programs. In other words, regarding Iranian WMD, given the excellent prospects that over the longer run Iran's policy will become less aggressive, delay means victory.

EXECUTIVE BRANCH OF THE ISLAMIC REPUBLIC

President
Muhammad Khatami

First Vice President
Hasan Habibi

Vice Presidents
Gholamreza Aqazadeh—*Atomic Energy (AEOI)*
Muhammad Baqerian—*Administrative and Recruiting*
Mas'umeh Ebtekar—*Environment Protection*
Muhammad Hashemi—*Executive Affairs*
Abdulvahab Musavi Lari—*Legal and Parliamentary Affairs*
Mustafa Hashemi Taba—*Physical Education*
Muhammad 'Ali Najafi—*Planning and Budget*
'Abdollah Nuri—*Adviser to the President*
Mir-Hosein Musavi—*Top Adviser to President*

Cabinet Ministers
'Isa Kalantari—*Agriculture*
Morteza Hajji—*Cooperatives*
Mustafa Mo'in—*Culture and Higher Education*
Adm. 'Ali Shamkhani—*Defense*
Muhammad Sa'idi-Kia—*Development*
Hosein Namazi—*Economic Affairs and Finance*
Hosein Mozaffar—*Education and Training*
Habibollah Bitaraf—*Energy*
Kamal Kharrazi—*Foreign Affairs*
Muhammad Farhadi—*Health*
'Ali 'Abdul'alizadeh—*Housing and Urban Development*
Gholamreza Shafe'i—*Industry*
Qorban 'Ali Dori Najafabadi—*Intelligence and Security*
Abdulvahab Musavi Lari—*Interior*
'Ata'ollah Mohajerani—*Islamic Culture and Guidance*
Isma'il Shushtari—*Justice*
Hosein Kamali—*Labor and Social Affairs*
Ishaq Jahangiri—*Mines and Metals*
Bijan Namdar Zanganeh—*Petroleum*
Mahmud Hojjati—*Roads and Transportation*
Muhammad Reza 'Aref—*Telecommunications*
Muhammad Shari'atmadar—*Trade*

11

Constitutional Responsibilities
of the Supreme Leader and the President

Article 110 (excerpts)

Following are the duties and powers of the Leadership [Supreme Leader]:

1. Delineation of the general policies of the Islamic Republic of Iran after consultation with the nation's Expediency Council.
2. Supervision over the proper execution of the general policies of the system.
3. Issuing decrees for national referenda.
4. Assuming supreme command of the armed forces.
5. Declaration of war and peace, and the mobilization of the armed forces.
6. Appointment, dismissal, and acceptance of resignation of:
   1. the *fuqaha'* [Islamic jurists] on the Guardian Council.
   2. the supreme judicial authority of the country.
   3. the head of the radio and television network of the Islamic Republic of Iran.
   4. the chief of the joint staff.
   5. the chief commander of the Islamic Revolutionary Guard Corps.
   6. the supreme commanders of the armed forces.
7. Resolving differences between the three wings of the armed forces and regulation of their relations.
8. Resolving the problems, which cannot be solved by conventional methods, through the nation's Expediency Council.

Article 113

After the office of Leadership, the President is the highest official in the country. His is the responsibility for implementing the Constitution and acting as the head of the executive, except in matters directly concerned with (the office of) the Leadership.

(From the Constitution of the Islamic Republic of Iran as translated by *Salam Iran* magazine online; for more information, see http://www.salamiran.org/IranInfo/State/Constitution/)

Chapter 2

WHITHER IRANIAN POLITICS?
The Khatami Factor

David Menashri

M uhammad Khatami won a landslide victory in Iran's presidential elections on May 23, 1997, and after being officially sworn in on August 4, he scored a stunning achievement with the August 20 approval by the Majlis (parliament) of all—even the most contentious—appointments for ministerial posts. These achievements were attributed to Khatami's popularity and believed to be an endorsement of greater openness. But the conservative faction remained strong and devoted to a revolutionary path, making the domestic power struggle seem far from settled and Iran's policies far from clear. The events preceding the elections, and the time that has elapsed since, sharpened the domestic power struggle, which is now being contested primarily between two main revolutionary camps: one pragmatic, the other conservative.[1]

That the elections took place on schedule and that the competing candidates were all loyal to basic revolutionary tenets attests to impressive continuity and a measure of political stability. If the election results marked a yearning for change, this yearning remained primarily within the framework of the revolutionary system—a call to modify policy, not to change the regime; to save the revolution, not to abandon the dogma entirely.

Yet, after almost two decades of Islamic rule, there was a growing sense that the revolution had not significantly eased— let alone solved—the social, economic, and political problems Iranians faced. Khatami's victory signaled growing popular disillusionment and disenchantment and a desire for the government to resolve the numerous difficulties and largely unfulfilled expectations, mainly of the *mostaz'afin* (underprivileged), youth, women, and the educated class. The vote was, in a way, a sign of protest—against the situation, the conservative elite in power, and uncompromising dogmatic devotion—with voters opting for more practical solutions, greater openness, pragmatism, and an increased role for Iran's civil society.

Khatami's election to the presidency was expected to turn into a momentous catalyst for policy change. A year later, with no substantial improvement in social and economic fields, domestic rivalries continue, with the pressure for conservatism confronting the drive for greater pragmatism. The direction of change, areas of reform, and rhythm of transformation are not yet clear. Moreover, the degree of power that Khatami's team holds cannot be determined with much certainty. Despite the ability in some areas to promote change, Khatami has faced significant obstacles when he has tried to implement certain programs. He has made some innovative and courageous statements advocating greater pragmatism, but the conservatives continue to have a grip on much of the government's power. As one Iranian source put it, since entering office, Khatami has hardly had "a crisis-free week."[2] Domestic rivalries reached a new peak around the first anniversary of the 1997 elections.

This chapter will point to elements of continuity, outline the stimuli for change in contrast to the factors that work to thwart new initiatives since the elections, and identify signs of change—as much as they can be discerned a year after Khatami's inauguration.

NEW PRESIDENT, SAME REVOLUTIONARY SYSTEM

Khatami's record and pragmatic statements raised expectations—in Iran and abroad—for dramatic policy change.

Khatami is not an "average mullah," one Western observer noted, but a president "with one foot in Western civilization."[3] He is not "the best representative of the ruling religious institution," one paper wrote, but "a different prototype [*namudaj*]," whose worldview differs "to a large extent" with that of the ruling system. A Lebanese scholar added that above all else he "is an intellectual."[4] Because of his focus on civil society and change *within* the revolutionary system, some Iranians have referred to him as "Ayatollah Gorbachev."[5] Others view him a "peaceful evolutionist" who could lead to an "Iranian-style perestroika."[6]

Despite the novelty of the election results and the expectations for future reforms, the basic framework of the *nezam* (Islamic revolutionary system) and the pivotal tenet of its creed (i.e., the concept of *velayat-e faqih*—the rule of the jurisconsult) remain intact. Khatami's presidency seems to constitute not a new regime but a fresh approach within the Islamic system: an attempt to fulfill revolutionary aspirations in a somewhat modified fashion. Significantly belittling the importance of the change, *Kayhan International* termed it a mere "orderly transition of power." Khatami's inauguration was "a change of president," it added, not (even) "a change of policy."[7] Yet, although in "no way, shape or form" can the election be viewed "as a vote to change the system," the election was, as a Western-trained Iranian academic said, "a vote for new ideas, new people, more responsive government."[8]

During his campaign, and since entering office, Khatami vowed to work within the system. The vision of Ayatollah Ruhollah Khomeini, he said, forms "the basis of our system" and the concept of velayat-e faqih is "the basis of our political and civil system." He pledged to "defend the values of the revolution."[9] The contention that his election was a sign of momentous change, *Kayhan* noted, ignored the fact that Khatami is a devout follower of Khomeini and a supporter of the revolution. Preferring to stress Khatami's past convictions rather than his newly formed stance, the paper added that "for a long time he has been recognized as an anti-American figure," and many of the political figures and factions that support him have "anti-American records." With these in mind, *Kayhan* wondered, how could he possibly "ignore the path and aspiration" of Khomeini, or initiate a compromise "between the revolution and its main enemy," the United States?[10]

Although his main rival, Majlis speaker 'Ali Akbar Nateq Nuri, was identified with the conservative establishment, Khatami too was supported by elements within the system— most prominently, 'Ali Akbar Hashemi Rafsanjani. Oddly, those resenting the situation voted for a candidate supported by the outgoing president. This also means that Khatami can be regarded as an outsider only to some degree. Moreover, whereas Khatami had the support of some pragmatic factions, such as the *khedmatgozaran-e sazandegi* (servants of reconstruction; usually referred to as the "modern right"), he was also supported by those usually known as radicals (or "left"). Most prominent among that latter group are the *Ruhaniyyun-e Mobarez-e Tehran* (the Combatant Clerics of Tehran), including former Interior Minister 'Ali Akbar Mohtashami and former Prosecutor General Muhammad Musavi Kho'iniha—people who have hitherto been among the most vigorous opponents of both rapprochement with the United States and *tahajom-e farhangi* ("Western onslaught").

Mohtashami, now backing Khatami, has been the figurehead of the radical approach. Only Iran's enemies, he once said, stress the primacy of economic reconstruction—as pragmatists often do—to divert attention from the more crucial issues of Iran's "political and cultural independence."[11] In his words: "If you set the economy as the principle and sacrifice everything at its altar, there would remain nothing by which you could be powerful, free, and independent."[12] Asserting that the restoration of ties with the United States would solve Iran's problems, he said, is tantamount to considering America "to be God on earth."[13] He criticized those raising such an idea as deluded—"bankrupt, Westernized, selfish elements" who are "bereft of intelligence and understanding." He maintained that rather than try to forge ties as the means to rehabilitate the economy, Iran should "vaccinate" itself against Western viruses.[14]

The pragmatists themselves have also remained generally loyal to the basic revolutionary convictions. The difference between the various domestic groups—although significant— is with respect to degree. As one of Khatami's ministers said, Iran should "leave the door open to allow a breeze through," but "not to let in a destructive storm."[15] The fundamental debate, therefore, is over what degree of openness turns a "breeze" into a "storm." Moreover, many of those who voted for Khatami meant mainly to signal displeasure with the ruling elite, rather than to endorse pragmatism or to identify fully with Khatami's particular philosophy. Like Khomeini in 1979, Khatami turned into a symbol that provided the people a renewed hope that his path would lead Iran to achieve hitherto unfulfilled revolutionary promises. Yet, the massive vote for Khatami is in itself insufficient to promote unqualified change. Policymaking continues to be subject to laborious bargaining or contests between the various power centers, of which the presidency is only one.

The head of the state is the *rahbar* (supreme leader)— Ayatollah 'Ali Khamene'i—not the president. In a way, however, Khatami's victory was a setback for Khamene'i. Not only did Khamene'i come close to openly endorsing Nateq Nuri, but being deeply involved in politics he could not escape responsibility for Iran's mounting difficulties. Moreover, he lacks the supreme religious authority to serve as the *marja'-e taqlid* (the source of imitation), which makes him even more vulnerable. It would be difficult to regard Khamene'i's rulings "as authoritative, binding, superior to those of other eminent jurists . . . and as the guidelines by which the state, society and individuals should conduct themselves."[16] Yet, his succession has inspired him "to be a genuine holy man."[17] Although he failed to gain full theological endorsement, his recognition as one of the *maraje'* and his actual position as rahbar bolster his authority.

Khamene'i's position in the revolutionary hierarchy limits Khatami's freedom, mainly as the rahbar does not share many of the president's convictions and in fact often identifies with the president's rivals. In Khamene'i's first meeting with the new government, on August 24, he cautioned it to preserve revolutionary values, resist the greed of foreign powers, and avoid hasty actions. His statements since (i.e., during the Organization of the Islamic Conference [OIC] summit in Tehran; see below) attest both to substantial differences with the president and to Khamene'i's determination to dictate politics. The appointment of 'Ali Akbar Velayati, who had been foreign minister since 1981, as his adviser for international affairs, further attests to the inherent tension between the desire for change and the struggle for continuity and points to the multiplicity of decision-making centers. *Iran News* wrote that this appointment "will guarantee continuance" of Iran's basic policy[18]—it certainly meant to guard against uncontrolled change.

More generally, in the absence of Khomeini's omnipotent command, factional rivalries at the highest echelons of power work to thwart decision making. In contrast to the shah's rule, says Shahram Chubin, Islamic Iran "makes policy in a more untidy and altogether less consistent manner." Its decision-making process is "subject to the play of domestic political forces" that "often pull in different directions."[19] Moreover, decisions default to the radical line, creating a built-in bias in favor of continued extremism. The religio-political structure and the multiplicity of power centers further block efforts to change. A range of state, clerical, and vested interests "embedded in Iran's complex structure of parallel policy-making and policy-vetting institutions" seem to oppose Khatami "tooth-and-nail," further limiting his ability to modify, or to fine-tune, foreign policy.[20] Khomeini's first prime minister, Mehdi Bazargan, complained in 1979 that his government held "a knife without a blade."[21] Khatami's election provided him with a mandate for a guarded change, but not carte blanche for unfettered openness or retreat from the revolutionary creed. It is not yet clear how much of a "blade" his knife carries.

The Majlis, hitherto a stronghold of conservatism, continues to strive for dominance and to check fresh initiatives, thus further limiting the president's freedom of action. Immediately following his defeat in the presidential election, Nateq Nuri was re-elected as speaker. The Majlis's approval of all of Khatami's nominees should therefore not be taken as either an *a priori* endorsement of their politics or a sign of uncritical approach. Since the early days of the revolution, the Majlis has proven a strong basis of power, and it is determined to preserve its status as the most important revolutionary institution after that of the supreme leader. The Majlis, too, represents the people. Its vote for the government did not indicate an acceptance of its politics. As Majlis member Ma'ruf Samadi said, "I am against the cabinet . . . but will vote for all of them."[22] True, there is a strong pro-Khatami nucleus in the Majlis. Some observers went so far as to view the 1996 Majlis elections as having "irrevocably changed" Iran's "internal political landscape," discerning "hints" of a "potential change" in its policy.[23] Still, the rahbar, the Majlis, and the judiciary—headed by Ayatollah Muhammad Yazdi—may block (or slow down) the president and his government's new initiatives. Yazdi's role in the detention of Tehran's mayor, Gholam-Hosein

Karbaschi, on April 4, 1998, was only one such example. A
more recent and blatant one was the Majlis interpellation of
Interior Minister 'Abdollah Nuri on June 21, 1998. The two, it
should be stressed, are among the main pillars of Khatami's
camp and his more resolute supporters.

Rafsanjani is another force with which Khatami has to
reckon. After eight years as speaker and two terms in the presidency, and given his revolutionary credentials, he maintains
significant influence. His post at the head of the Expediency
Council—to which Khamene'i recently gave more powers—
gives him key decision-making authority in disputes between
the legislative and the executive branch. Also, Rafsanjani may
have the loyalty of many of Khatami's ministers and a few
vice presidents whom the former president first promoted to
their current rank. Some of them played central roles in the
formation of the khedmatgozaran-e sazandegi. Thus, at this
initial stage, Rafsanjani's support seems crucial for Khatami's
success. But so far the former president seems to be sitting on
the fence. He has not put his full weight behind the president,
though when it appeared important enough—such as to secure Karbaschi's release—Rafsanjani and Khatami have been
in the same camp.

Although being an establishment "outsider" was an asset
during his campaign, Khatami's lack of an independent power
base now that he is in office has presented him with strong
challenges to advancing his promises of reform. Much of his
freedom of action depends on the other power centers: the
rahbar, the faction-ridden Majlis, the revolutionary organizations (the Revolutionary Guard and the Basij militia) and foundations (such as the *Bonyad-e Mostaz'afin* and the *Bonyad-e
Shahid*), and a range of vested interests. At this stage, it seems
that the conservatives possess disproportionately more power
in the ruling institutions than among the civil society. Whereas
former Soviet leader Mikhail Gorbachev seized control of the

party and the state when he became the Communist Party's secretary general and president, Khatami has to share power. All these significantly restrict his freedom of action in many vital policy areas.

That the revolution has already deviated from many of its ideological convictions makes it even harder to retreat from the remaining elements of its creed—such as establishing ties with the United States or changing its attitude toward Israel. That such issues have already turned into symbols of the revolution makes such a sea-change even more arduous—a retreat from them may now appear as an open admission of failure or, as former Foreign Minister Velayati has put it, lead to the defeat of Iran's revolutionary myths (see below).

Finally, the objective difficulties of solving the mounting social and economic difficulties—among others—would be enormous for any government, let alone given the circumstances under which the new team operates.

Popular expectations provided Khatami with decisive support but also imposed a heavy burden, as Iranians and foreign observers alike seem to expect immediate action and instant results. Khatami, the *Financial Times* rightly observed, carries "a heavy burden of expectation."[24] Expectations "rise high" added *Kayhan International*.[25] Faced with a similar challenge, then–Prime Minister Bazargan appealed in 1979: "I am not another [Imam] 'Ali." He was not "a bulldozer," he said, "crushing all obstacles in its path," but rather "a delicate car" capable of moving only on good roads: "You should pave the way for me."[26] Whether Khatami can gain the required assistance remains to be seen.

KHATAMI'S SEARCH FOR AN EQUILIBRIUM

Despite all the difficulties inherent in seeking a substantial and immediate breakthrough, the current conditions seem propitious for change: The revolution has matured, the people are more discontented, and the mood calls for pragmatism, even at the expense of some retreat from established dogma. By now, many—and constantly growing numbers of—revolutionaries have realized that a measure of pragmatism is essential to resolve the mounting problems and to secure the regime's longevity and stability. Khatami received a mandate for change and seems aware of the need to do so. His election campaign, and his statements since taking over, suggest that he is both determined to make good on his pledges and confident that his program is the best way to advance the revolutionary goals.

The Majlis's approval of all of Khatami's cabinet nominees strengthened his mandate. Khatami described his team as a cohesive, harmonious, and capable collective, combining the experience, innovation, and new thinking that can enable the government "to fulfill our religious, revolutionary, and national obligations."[27] Much like the outgoing government, it is a highly professional team of technocrats with strong revolutionary credentials. Most of them have served in previous governments—half of them were ministers and vice presidents—or had held prominent positions in the former administration (i.e., as provincial governor or as member of the Majlis, Council of Experts, or Expediency Council). Two of Iran's vice presidents—Hasan Habibi and Muhammad Hashemi, Rafsanjani's brother—retained their post from the last administration, and another, Muhammad 'Ali Najafi, was a minister in Rafsanjani's cabinet.

Khatami's nomination of highly controversial candidates to some key posts attests to his determination to blaze his own trail. 'Ata'ollah Mohajerani, minister of Islamic guidance, had antagonized conservatives by criticizing the restriction of freedoms and supporting a constitutional amendment to allow Rafsanjani to run for a third term—the latter move was viewed as an attempt to block Nateq Nuri and the conservatives from gaining the presidency. Above all, he wrote a famous article in

Ettela'at in 1990, pointing to the advisability of dialogue with the United States.[28] 'Abdollah Nuri, minister of the interior, stood behind Khatami throughout his campaign and vehemently criticized the conservatives for monopolizing power.[29] Castigating the conservatives' campaign against "liberals," he then said that the interests of the revolution compel endorsing more liberal policies.[30] Kamal Kharrazi, minister of foreign affairs, was blamed for having spent too long in the United States, first as a student and later as UN ambassador, and thus for being influenced by American culture. True, Khatami was not entirely "liberal" with his appointments. Although he appointed a woman, Ma'sumeh Ebtekar, as vice president—for which he did not need Majlis approval—he did not nominate any women to the position of cabinet minister.[31] Yet, the approval of all, even the most contentious appointments—often after fierce criticism—was substantial proof of Khatami's strength.[32]

More important, by Iranian standards Khatami *is* liberal[33] and seems determined to pursue his pragmatic policy. Although serving as the minister of Islamic guidance for a decade, he has been outside government since 1992 and has gained a reputation for supporting greater openness. During his "exile" as the director of the National Library, he maintained contact with intellectuals and artists, supporting and encouraging them. For him, "liberal" is not a derogatory term. In contrast to Nateq Nuri's dogmatic devotion, Khatami supports relative openness, advocating greater freedom, flexibility, care for the youth, women's rights, social welfare, and economic rehabilitation, which also necessitates a more pragmatic attitude toward the outside world.

As Nateq Nuri turned into the symbol of the establishment and conservatism, Khatami became the symbol of pragmatism, openness, and change. During the campaign, therefore, as much as Khatami labored to stress his revolutionary credentials and devotion to Khomeini's creed, Nateq Nuri worked to shake his reputation as an uncompromising ideologue. Yet, the two turned into symbols of two different currents: Khatami became a symbol of an establishment outsider, who would promote reform, change, and openness; he represented the hope for a brighter future and was considered the one who would "shake things up." Nateq Nuri came to represent the conservative establishment, which had failed to fulfill the revolutionary pledges, and was a symbol of the status quo.[34]

In representing the conservative approach, Nateq Nuri maintained that building bridges and paving highways—usually symbols of reconstruction and the aim of the pragmatists—had nothing to do with "preserving revolutionary values." If infrastructure projects were the yardstick by which Islamic governments were measured, he once said, Malaysia would have been a better model of an Islamic state.[35] He rejected any sign of foreign influence as Western "cultural onslaught." For him, the gulf between Iran and the United States was unbridgeable, for "our struggle against America has its origin in our ideology." Inasmuch as America by "its nature" was domineering, Iran's struggle against it would continue.[36] Similarly, arguing that Israel's vision was to realize "the Nile-to-Euphrates dream," he said defending Palestine is a religious duty.[37]

Khatami supported greater openness in domestic politics and viewed outside influence as unavoidable, and even advantageous, provided Iran could preserve its identity and independence. Resigning from his ministerial post in 1992, he warned that if the path of the revolution were not modified, Iran would see "the beginning of a dangerous trend."[38] He feared that the political, social, and economic realities in Iran could spill far from its borders to discourage Islamists elsewhere, and even endanger Islam.[39] His aim was not to abandon the revolutionary path, but to return it to its appropriate tracks, maintaining dogma and advancing the welfare of the country and the people, thus not only serving but possibly saving the revolution.

In Khatami's view, the "gravest problem" facing the world of Islam is that "*thaqafatuna* [our culture] belongs to a civilization that has long passed away, while we live under the impact of a new [Western] civilization" with which we have to comply.[40] For centuries, Islam had not been involved in running the state.[41] The West is the birthplace of the new civilization, he maintained, and civilizations influence each other.[42] This is an age of "the dominance and entrenchment" of Western civilization, "intellectually, morally, and technologically." The West has "made great strides in science, politics, and social regulation," he said, though it is "worn out and senile." Iran has to understand the West "correctly and comprehensively," to "judge it fairly and objectively" and "use its strengths," while "staying clear of its defects by relying on our revolution's values."[43] The "give-and-take among civilizations is the norm of history."[44] Knowledge of Western culture and civilization, he said, is a historical necessity.[45]

Muslims, Khatami said, should look at the West "with a neutral outlook," devoid of sentiments, to avoid its dangers but to benefit from its human achievement. They should strive to reestablish their great civilization, not by remaining in the past, but by striving forward to new horizons.[46] In addition to its political "face," the West also has an intellectual dimension, with liberalism as its cornerstone.[47] He rejected the views of conservatives, who wish to return to the past, as well as those of the *mabhurun* (those intoxicated by the West), suggesting instead an "intellectual approach": selective borrowing. This, he said, necessitates a new look into Muslim sources, including the Qur'an and the Sunna, and taking into account Iran's present needs.[48]

Basing his argument on Khomeini's verdicts, Khatami

stressed the centrality of *maslehat* (interests) in shaping politics: "the best interests of Islam . . . our Islamic country . . . [and] of the people." According to Khomeini, he said, proper governance is one of the primary commands of Islam.[49] His accent on "the interests of the system" or "proper governance" sought to justify some dogmatic deviations. It should be noted that, from the same premise, Khomeini in 1987–1988 went as far as sanctioning the state's authority even to "destroy a mosque" or to suspend the exercise of the "five pillars of faith," if state interest so dictates.[50] Rafsanjani then interpreted Khomeini's guidelines: The "law should follow Islamic doctrine" but, if necessary, "priority will be given to government decision over doctrine."[51] This in a nutshell was Khatami's basic concept.

Khatami was aware that "chanting slogans" alone could not secure Iran's revolutionary goals. Faced with a similar challenge by his own dogmatic rival, Rafsanjani in 1992 had called upon his challengers—some of whom now support Khatami—to substitute *sho'ur* (intelligence) for *sho'ar* (slogans).[52] Similarly, Khatami reiterated the need to abandon empty slogans, opting instead for practical solutions. In his view, demonstrating economic and political strength will advance Iran's revolutionary values far more than slogans can.[53] Moreover, in a world of "computers, communication networks, satellites, and sound waves," Khatami has said there is nothing wrong with "utilizing the experience of other human communities," as long as it is not done to "imitate them blindly" or to abandon Iranians' "own identity," but rather to borrow "the good points of other cultures" and thus to "enrich our own culture."[54]

Khatami's pragmatic outlook also encompassed foreign ties. In his view, "foreign policy does not mean guns and rifles," but making use of all legitimate "international means" to convince others.[55] Iran, he said, wants relations with all the nations "which respect our independence, dignity, and interests."

If Iran does not have relations "with an aggressive and bully-ing country" such as the United States, this is because of that country's failure to "respect those principles" and because it put itself "at the head of the aggressors and conspirators against us." In a mixture of pragmatism and revolutionary devotion, he added: Iran "will not interfere in the affairs of others"; nev-ertheless, defending "the deprived and oppressed" and "free-dom-seeking countries," throughout the world, especially the Palestinians, is Iran's "Islamic and revolutionary obligation."[56]

PRAGMATIC STATEMENTS, EXTREMIST REPLIES

Since his election, Khatami has made several courageous prag-matic statements. True, he has often fenced such statements with significant conditions and declarations of dogmatic de-votion. But, in all, they attest to an aptitude for change and an impressive degree of persistence. Previously, when faced with criticism, Iranian pragmatists usually retreated after making one step forward; Khatami, although moving forward slowly, has hitherto not pulled back.

When formally sworn in, Khatami offered dialogue as a mechanism for removing misunderstandings between nations. Only mutual respect and common interests could lead to a fruit-ful dialogue; revolutionary principles, he added, lead Iran "to maintain good relations with all nations except Israel." He re-iterated: "My government considers dialogue between civili-zations . . . essential, and will avoid any action or behavior causing tension." He also vowed to "resist any power wishing to exercise dominance over us," and to support the deprived, particularly the Palestinians.[57] In his speech at the OIC on De-cember 9, 1997, he added: "The replication of the old [Islamic] civilization is neither possible . . . nor desirable"; this is "the era of preponderance" of Western civilization, "whose accom-plishments are not few, and yet, whose negative consequences, particularly for non-Westerners, are plentiful." Through dialogue Iran should open the way toward mutual understanding and genuine peace, he said, "based on the realization of the rights of all nations."[58] In a subsequent press conference on December 14, Khatami said, "instead of using the language of force, people should use the language of reason and logic to speak to each other." He added: "I want to have a philosophical and historical interchange with the American people and believe that whatever intellectual interchanges go ahead, the world will achieve peace."[59] In an interview on CNN in January, he further voiced mild language, signaling willingness to open a new chapter in the Iranian–U.S. relationship.[60]

Prominent Iranian officials, taking his hint, followed suit. Muhammad Javad Larijani, a Majlis deputy for Tehran, said reducing tensions with the United States is in Iran's "national interests." After all, many countries fight with each other but continue to maintain ties. But, he said, "many of our friends oppose this view."[61] Foreign Minister Kharrazi, reiterating that the ball was in the American court, added, "We are ready to work with all nations, provided they are ready to establish their relations with us based on mutual respect."[62] *Salam* (hitherto known for its fierce anti-American stance) has often published readers' claims in favor of dialogue and has voiced a more moderate tone itself. As one reader asked, would it be more difficult to change the anti-American line than to retreat from the anti-Iraqi slogans? Why are relations with Britain acceptable, another asked, while dialogue with the United States is not? If the Americans have usurped Iran's rights, another asked, is it not better to talk with them to regain these rights?[63] Reiterating similar questions, *Salam* wondered: Is there any doubt that many Iranians support dialogue, and that their number is constantly growing?[64] Iran, it said, should not be terrified by an offer of dialogue.[65]

Occasionally, and mainly to a domestic audience, Khatami has sounded as extremist as his rivals. Thus, addressing school children in November 1997, on the anniversary of the 1979 seizure of the American embassy and hostages, he castigated the "misguided and expansionist" American politicians, who "place their nation's resources and interests against other nations." Making a distinction between Iran's objection to American policies and "our opinion of the American nation," he said that, to "make up for the past," American politicians "must apologize" to the Iranian nation. Unfortunately, he added, U.S. enmities continue—"in a terrified and mindless way." It is as if Washington "considers fighting the Iranian nation" as its "main mission," he said,[66] adding that the key to resolving the problem is in the hands of the Clinton administration, but unfortunately "we do not see" any positive signs from Washington. U.S. policy, he said, has always been hostile toward the revolution, the Iranian people, and their interests.[67] Even such radical statements, however, could not curtail the importance of the newly formed trend and the improved atmosphere in bilateral relations (see below).

Still, whatever pragmatic statements Khatami made were "balanced" by radical expressions by Khamene'i and other conservative figures. Thus, as the *Los Angeles Times* wrote, the OIC put on "display the widening political divisions" between the "dogmatic clerics" and their "more pragmatic rivals"; whereas Khatami endorsed dialogue to achieve "deep-rooted understanding," Khamene'i delivered "a fiery speech that boiled over with hostility toward the West, especially the United States."[68] Khamene'i continued with his customary harsh tone, blaming the hidden hands of arrogance for keeping Muslims apart. Western civilization, he said, "is directing everyone toward materialism while money gluttony and carnal desires are made the greatest aspirations." The West, he said, in "its all-rounded invasion," has "targeted our Islamic faith and character." It has "intensely and persistently exported to our countries the culture of laxness and disregard for religion and ethics."[69] Khamene'i's international affairs adviser, Velayati, similarly continued to adhere to the customary line of his sixteen years in the foreign ministry. Mere talk of dialogue, he said, only serves the enemy. Blaming the advocates of such a policy as "stupid" or "dependent on foreigners," he warned that such a policy might lead to the defeat of the revolutionary myths of Islamic resistance.[70] *Iran News*, commenting on President Bill Clinton's expressed hope in 1997 that Khatami's election may "bode well for the future," noted that, had the American president and his aides studied the basics of the Islamic revolution, Khatami's presidency would not have seemed so "intriguing" and "fascinating." As the United States has failed to show any goodwill, the paper said, the two governments are "treading on opposite paths that will never meet."[71] *Jomhuri-ye Islami,*[72] *Resalat,*[73] and *Kayhan*[74] often supported this line.

The American request that Khatami's mild words be matched by deeds further infuriated Iranians. "What is most important are actions, not words," said Secretary of State Madeleine Albright after Khatami's election. More specifically, the United States laid down three benchmarks to test Iran's actual approach: "to support the Middle East peace process, not to be involved in creating and possessing weapons of mass destruction, and not supporting terrorism."[75] In response, *Kayhan International* wrote that the Clinton administration's "anti-Iran rhetoric" meant that Washington "is not sincere, neither is it serious." It is up to the U.S. administration "to take that initiative," the paper continued, such as by releasing frozen Iranian assets.[76] Washington's preconditions prove, added *Kayhan,* that Americans simply want to impose their "arrogant conditions" on Iran, to "turn Iran into a submissive, useless, and abject entity."[77] Iran's conservative press dismissed those supporting such a dialogue as misguided, superficial, and naive—people who fail to understand the enemy's main intentions.[78]

In all, however, a significant change had been registered in the atmosphere of the bilateral relationship even before Albright's speech in June 1998 (see below). Among the obstacles were the sentiments—on both sides—against each other, and the fact that animosity toward Washington had long become such a major symbol of the Islamic revolution, which was "raised . . . to a near religion."[79] In the past, willing to prove their revolutionary devotion, some pragmatists even waved the remaining anti-American and anti-Israeli "flags," rather than bring them down. At this stage, it seems that one of the "flag bearers"—Khatami—is trying to separate the two and lower the anti-American banner.

The practical steps toward dialogue were less impressive, with both sides claiming that the ball was in the other's court. Tehran demanded that Washington supplement its statements with actual proof of goodwill (such as unfreezing Iranian assets); Washington put forward significant preconditions and difficult benchmarks. True, some important strides were made, such as the visit to Iran of an American wrestling team in February 1998, the visit of Iranian wrestlers to the United States in April; and the Iran–U.S. World Cup soccer game in France in June. Important statements by Secretary of State Albright on June 17 and later by President Clinton infused new hope for rapprochement. In all, the atmosphere for expanding academic, economic, and other ties has improved, and there is a sense that a breakthrough is possible, but the wounds of the past and the lack of mutual trust continue to imperil mutual relations.

Whereas there has been some change in the pragmatists' approach to the United States, the harsh anti-Israeli attitude continues, shared by pragmatists and conservatives alike. Reiterating Iran's opposition to the peace process, Khatami pledged following his election not take action to disrupt it. Iran is interested in "peace and tranquility," he said, but this can be achieved only with the restoration of the legal rights of the Palestinians. Iran, he added, reserves "the right to comment on what we consider as right and what we perceive as unjust."[80]

Yet, the fact remained that even when the Palestinians chose to pursue the peace process, the general Iranian tone remained extremely critical. At the OIC, Khatami said that genuine peace can be established "only through the realization of all the legitimate rights of the Palestinian people, including the inalienable right to self-determination, return of refugees, [and] liberation of [all] the occupied territories." Yet, "the hegemonic, racist, aggressive and violent nature of the Zionist regime," manifested in "the systematic and gross violation of international law, pursuit of state terrorism, and development of weapons of mass destruction, seriously threatens peace and security in the region."[81] He again said that Iran opposed the peace process because it "is not a just one" and is thus doomed to fail. Arabs dealing with Israel, he said, have realized by now that "they are dealing with a racist, terrorist, and expansionist regime."[82] To children of Lebanese martyrs, Khatami described Israel as "the most prominent manifestation of international terrorism."[83] Reiterating Iran's commitment to support the deprived, he asked: "Which tribe is more deprived than the oppressed and outcast people of Palestine? Which factor is stronger than the racist, Zionist regime in creating tension?" In his view, the "root of tension" is Israel and the cause of tension is America's support for that "racist, bullying regime, that focal point of state terrorism."[84] Meeting Hamas leader Shaykh Ahmad Yasin in May 1998, Khatami expressed hope that someday a Palestinian government will be established in Palestine. Terming Zionism a "continuation of fascism," Khatami added: "I am sure that the future will be in favor of the righteous and to the benefit of the Palestinian resistant people."[85]

Khamene'i was even more radical. At the OIC he described the peace process as "unjust, arrogant, contemptuous," and "illogical."[86] *Kayhan International* then claimed, that Israel is the only country "which is not recognized" by Iran, because Israel has usurped Palestinians rights. It recited the customary line: "Israel should be erased from the map of the Middle East."[87] Even "at the cost of its own national interests," *Iran News* wrote, Iran "can never compromise" on the question of Palestine. Support for the liberation of Palestine has been at the core of Iran's policy, ever since Khomeini "christened the Zionist regime a 'cancerous tumor' that must be eradicated from the body of the *ummah*."[88] Many statements and commentaries, often basing themselves on Khomeini's creed, reiterated this attitude.[89] More important, no substantial change has been noticed in Iran's support for Hizballah or Islamist movements, although some signs of a milder tone have recently been detected. These could be discerned from the conservatives' criticism, rather than from direct and clear statements. *Jomhuri-ye Islami* thus urged officials to avoid vague statements and to adhere to the clear and accepted policy—that the Zionist regime is not legitimate and that this cancerous growth must be uprooted from the foundation.[90]

Radical sentiments were expressed even more vigorously during the visits to Iran of Shaykh Yasin and of Roger Garaudy, the French author, in April–May 1998. Meeting Garaudy, Khamene'i said Iran's campaign against the United States and Zionism is founded on Islamic and logical principles. Pointing to similarities between the Zionists and the Nazis, he castigated Western governments: "On the one hand, they deplore the racial behavior of the Nazis toward the Jews and on the other they support the Zionists who have the same behavior as that of the Nazis." Supporting the Zionists is as bad as supporting Nazi Germany and Hitler, he stated.[91] Meeting Shaykh Yasin, Khamene'i described Palestine as the frontline of Islam's war against infidelity and vowed to continued decisive support: Iran will "not recognize the usurper Zionist government even for one hour and will continue to struggle against this cancerous growth."[92] Animosity to Israel thus remains the main issue over which there has been some kind of agreement within the rival Iranian camps.

A YEAR LATER

A year after the elections, domestic rivalries further intensified, reaching a new peak. This could be deduced from the terms they used to denounce each other; for example, there were references equating Khatami's rule to that of the ousted President Abul-Hasan Bani Sadr,[93] and allusions to his tenure as chicken pox or "a sudden accident which will cool down quickly."[94] Domestic opponents have even been alluded to as "Yazid" (the notorious Caliph charged with the massacre of Imam Hosein in Karbala in A.D. 680).[95] Yahya Rahim Safavi, commander of the Revolutionary Guard, called Khatami's supporters "diseased people" whose plague is well known to the authorities, adding that the Revolutionary Guard is even ready to decapitate and cut out the tongues of political opponents.[96]

The challenges were stern and domestic differences multifaceted. Here only four developments will be discussed: the challenge posed by Ayatollah Hosein 'Ali Montazeri to the basic revolutionary concept of the velayat-e faqih; the detention on April 4 and subsequent trial of Karbaschi, the popular mayor of Tehran; the interpellation and dismissal on June 21 of Interior Minister Nuri; and the reaction to the June 17 statement made by Secretary of State Albright. They illustrate the depth of the Iranian dichotomy as well as its political implications.

The issue of qualification for religio-political guardianship, which presented the regime with a serious ideological challenge with significant political implications, arose with unprecedented magnitude following, and not unrelated to, the presidential elections.

Montazeri continued to challenge the very philosophy of the Islamic regime and protested against the harsh realities established under the Islamic rule.[97] In a Friday sermon on November 14, he went as far as claiming that the role of the velayat-e faqih is not to be "in charge of everything," but rather, like the Prophet, "to supervise" the affairs of society to make sure they do not deviate from Islamic rules. Moreover, whereas the essence of velayat-e faqih is a just, learned, and competent jurisprudent, Montazeri pointed out, Khamene'i does not even have the right to issue a *fatwa*. Arguing that the term republic "meant the people's rule," Montazeri urged people to be active in politics and prevent the misuse of the rulers' power. Montazeri reported that he had sent a message to Khatami to urge him to be more assertive, saying that, were he in Khatami's position, he would go to the supreme leader and point out that more than 22 million people had voted for him, supporting his own line, which they knew was different from that of Khamene'i. If Khatami's conditions were not accepted, Montazeri said, he (Khatami) should resign.[98] Montazeri's attack coincided with similar charges made by Ayatollah Ahmad Azeri-Qomi, who issued a strong statement on November 19, opening with the theme "God is the avenger." He tellingly cited another tradition: Anyone who witnesses an unjust ruler and keeps silent is a partner in his crimes. Leaving no room for error, he went on to assert that "Khamene'i kills the pious and tortures them, reviles the good and [sends them] to slaughter, and continues usurping the Office of the Guardian." People may not remain idle while witnessing "such crimes," he said, but must "perform the duty of preventing evil."[99]

The official response to such vociferous criticism was harsh, revealing the depth of the challenge. In announcing on November 21 that this "conspiracy" had its origins in outside agents, Yazdi, the head of the judiciary, added that whoever claimed that governance was not part of Islam and that the Prophet engaged only in consultation, did not know Islam. He wondered how people could depict the *velayat* as "rule over people who are insane and imbecilic." Yazdi portrayed Khamene'i as "both the leader of the state and the *marja'* of [all] world Muslims."[100] The chairman of the Council of Experts, 'Ali Meshkini, accused Montazeri of inciting the president against the leader, adding: "Our leader is fully eligible and his leadership is faultless."[101] Former minister of intelligence Muhammad Muhammadi Reyshahri added that Montazeri's statement was in fact a call for revolt.[102] On November 26, Khamene'i himself censured Montazeri and Azeri-Qomi, although not by name. He said that the enemy, having tried all sorts of methods to confront the revolution, now turned to "a more effective method, . . . targeting the leadership." Those who incite by creating discord have "committed acts of treason." If "those actions are illegal, which they are, if they are acts of treason, which they are," then the legal authorities must put them on trial for implementing the foreigners' conspiracies.[103]

Finally, the conservative elite published a previously undisclosed letter that Khomeini had written to Montazeri in 1989, which set out the reasons why Montazeri was not qualified to be Khomeini's successor. In this letter, Khomeini charged him with serving as a mouthpiece of hypocrites, termed him simple-minded and one who is "easily provoked," and forbade him to engage in politics. Montazeri's deeds were tantamount to treason, and Khomeini advised him to confess to all his sins and mistakes.[104] *Jomhuri-ye Islami* concluded: Any person who claims to follow Khomeini must prove his sincerity today; otherwise, the way remains open "for the enemies of Khomeini's aspirations."[105] Pro- and anti-Montazeri demonstrations reached new peaks in the spring of 1998 and often led to violent clashes.

Although the criticism of Montazeri was almost universally harsh, a few responses were more moderate. In an open letter to Khatami, A'zam Taleqani (daughter of the late Ayatollah Mahmud Taleqani) condemned the widespread attitude toward Montazeri. She considered Montazeri's remarks to be part of a scholarly–religious and sociological debate, but she said he had crossed a red line that unfortunately had released unusual propagandistic impulses.[106] Others hinted at a "great deal of coordination" between Montazeri and Professor 'Abdul-Karim Soroush, or in any event between their views.[107]

Iranian intellectuals continued to lead the struggle for freedom. Students proved very active, demonstrating forceful support for the president and his pragmatic politics all over the country and throughout the year—especially at the universities of Tehran, Tabriz, and Isfahan, and particularly around the anniversary of his election, in late May and early June 1998. Newspapers such as the new daily, *Jame'e* (later closed and replaced by *Tous*), made penetrating arguments against the government. The main challenges were raised by intellectuals such as Soroush, who were outside the establishment.[108] With all their differences, some of their main claims were not totally unrelated to those of Montazeri. According to Soroush, the "ideologization of religion" is the beginning of its vulgarization and leads to its deterioration. Religion, he said, is richer, more comprehensive, and more humane than ideology. His views, too, included an implicit attack on the institution of the velayat-e faqih. He continued to raise such views and was supported by many intellectuals. Generally speaking, both groups—dissident clerics and lay intellectuals—were closer to Khatami than to Khamene'i.

A second development occurred early in April, when Tehran's mayor was detained for charges of embezzlement and misconduct. Karbaschi was released after eleven days and was later put on trial. His opponents insisted that an official charged with corruption—no matter his rank, past services or political affiliation—has to stand trial, and that Karbaschi's achievements during nine years of mayorship were no grounds to waive the charges against him. They accused his supporters of deliberately politicizing the case to tarnish the authenticity of the trial.[109] The head of the administrative tribunal, Gholam-Hosein Mohseni, claimed that the detention was not politically motivated and promised a trial regardless of any political row.[110] Majlis deputy Muhammad Reza Bahonar asked those who chant slogans about the rule of law to be tolerant of its being applied to the mayor. It was Karbaschi's supporters, he said, who turned the trial into a political issue.[111] His colleague 'Ali Zadsar Jirofti added that not only the mayor but his superiors "are also guilty"—not only did Rafsanjani not stop him, but the former president indirectly encouraged the mayor, he said. If one were to review the performance of those politicians who advocate democracy, he added, one would realize that they are absolute dictators. "Karbaschi and his gang are an example of these authoritarian politicians."[112]

Supporters of Karbaschi viewed the whole affair as a political trial aimed at undermining Khatami's government. They argued that charges against him were leveled because of his role in the khedmatgozaran-e sazandegi and in Khatami's election, and that the trial was organized by the right wing to revenge their electoral defeat. They said the mayor, who in less than a decade transformed the appearance of Tehran, deserved praise, not punishment. They charged that, unwilling to relinquish power, the right wing turned against Karbaschi, was trying to bring down Nuri, and may target next Mohajerani—the pillars of the Khatami administration.[113] Majlis deputy Muhammad Baqer Musavi Jahan-Abad found it strange that "one of the strongest and dedicated" managers has been accused of mismanagement.[114] Fa'ezeh Hashemi, Rafsanjani's daughter, similarly said that, by bringing Karbaschi to trial, the faction that lost the election was seeking to take revenge.[115] "This affair has a political color to it," she said, adding, "Karbaschi's arrest is a blow to democracy, political and cultural reform in Iran."[116]

To show his support, 'Abdollah Nuri called upon Karbaschi's family upon his return from Saudi Arabia, bringing them a piece of the drapery of the Holy Ka'bah. It was sad, he said, that the arrest—instead of bringing Karbaschi under question—has put the judiciary under question. People should be tried for their offenses, he said, not for their competency, merit, boldness, and courage.[117] He called Karbaschi a "national hero," with his audience responding: "free the Amir Kabir."[118] Ayatollah Seyyed Jalal ul-din Taheri, the Friday prayer leader of Isfahan, maintained that Karbaschi's detention was directly related to the epic of the second of Khordad— May 23, Khatami's election—and "is 100 percent politically motivated."[119] Sadeq Khalkhali, the former revolutionary prosecutor, similarly added: "A group of people, falling back on partisanship," wished "to make up for this [presidential] defeat by arresting Karbaschi."[120]

The third development to arise, on June 10, was the demand by thirty-one Majlis deputies that Nuri be interpellated; they claimed that his tenure in the interior ministry was "detrimental to tranquility and stability in the country."[121] Nuri was an even more important target than was Karbaschi, because of his governmental post (in charge of elections, political activities, and licensing demonstrations), his open and unequivocal endorsement of liberalism, his support for the president, and, as shown earlier, his support for Karbaschi.

Nuri's supporters also pointed to the factional motivations behind this move. The leader of the *Majma'-e Hezbollah* Majlis faction, Majid Ansari, called the right wing the interpellation's

main architects.[122] A *Salam* commentary argued that the thirty-
one Majlis members, failing to grasp the message of the popular vote, were "lining up" against the "creators of the epic of 2
Khordad"—that is, "the people." Who should be interpellated?
it asked, a person who has issued a permit for a political gathering, or those "who have adopted a tacitly approving silence
in the face of the ruthless attack waged against the gathering
by a notorious gang wielding clubs, wearing knuckle-dusters
and even carrying tear gas canisters?"[123] *Mobin* added: "It is
not the interior minister alone" who is being attacked, but "the
president himself, the entire cabinet, all the forces and groups
who support Khatami and all those millions who created the
epic event of 2 Khordad."[124]

Khatami, vowing to respect the Majlis decision, still considered Nuri's service in the cabinet "beneficial and useful."
He thanked Nuri and his colleagues at the Interior Ministry
who "have bravely taken important actions to further the security and political development of the country," vowing that
whoever his successor be, he will follow Nuri's path. He promised that the government would make good use of Nuri's capabilities and experience[125] and thus made him a vice president.

It was exactly when such developments were taking place,
on June 17, 1998, that Secretary of State Albright delivered a
mild statement regarding Iran. Her speech and President
Clinton's subsequent statement had an exceptionally moderate tone, but they were immediately turned into another issue
for Iranian domestic controversy. Albright's statement was important primarily for what it mentioned. Her reference to the
Islamic regime (perceived as a hint that the United States recognized the regime's legitimacy and was willing to negotiate
with it) and the reference to security in "the Persian Gulf,"
sounded positive to Iranian ears. She stressed the "signs of
change" in Iran since Khatami's election (his gestures of goodwill, combating drug smuggling, and attempts at mediating in

Afghanistan) and added that the United States "fully respects Iran's sovereignty" and that the two countries "are now focused on the future." She added, "We are ready to explore further ways to build mutual confidence and avoid misunderstandings." Obviously, "two decades of mistrust cannot be erased overnight," she said, and the gap may "remain wide," but she added that it is now "time to test the possibilities for bridging this gap." The speech also lacked the customary reference to Iran as rouge and outlaw state. While stating that there is much more that Iran must do to prove its trustworthiness (i.e., on the issues of terrorism and human rights), Albright left the door open to improved relations.[126] No major breakthrough was expected instantly. As State Department spokesman James Rubin said on June 18, the United States expects reaction "over time," not "overnight."[127] Yet, the timing of the American gesture, in the midst of growing tension between the domestic camps, was somewhat problematic for Khatami and his colleagues. Still, given that it took the United States a few months to respond to Khatami's January CNN interview, this is another important step in the slow-motion dialogue—helping to smooth the atmosphere between Khatami and the White House but simultaneously exacerbating the ongoing dispute within Iran.

For the conservatives this was no less a crucial issue than the controversies over domestic issues.[128] The Iranian response to Albright's speech was thus similarly divided: Some vehemently rejected any possible rapprochement,[129] others sounded more forthcoming.[130] Interestingly, supporters of rapprochement expressed their views more openly than ever before. *Jame'e* criticized Iran's isolationist policy, asking why Iran demands that Washington meet certain preconditions prior to having relations with Tehran, when no similar attitude was applied to other former foes, such as Iraq. Iran adopted an extremist, rejectionist approach, it added, which was supposed to earn the country prestige, because Tehran feared that a withdrawal from such a policy would cost Iran its last card.[131]

CONCLUSIONS

Khatami's election attests to growing disillusionment in Iran and a popular urge for change. The election results may be viewed as a stiff warning to the leaders of the revolution, but also as a renewed chance to prove that the revolution possesses the cure for the basic social, economic, and political problems that had led to the revolution in the first place. Although some relaxation in the cultural and political atmosphere has been noticed in the last year, the domestic struggle for power continued. More important, the domestic social and economic difficulties remained as pressing as before. This has now become the daunting challenge for Khatami. The popular vote was clear. What it meant in terms of politics is more difficult to discern. While "the old guard continues to dominate," clearly, a "smell of change is in the air."[132] A year after the election, however, no breakthrough can yet be traced. Although new alignments have manifest themselves, the results of the struggle to shape the revolutionary policy are not clear.

Rather than any ideological conviction, the main stimuli for change rest in the growing domestic difficulties. The experience of the last year attests to Khatami's awareness of the challenge and his eagerness for change. But it also attests to the significant limitations upon his ability to produce a dramatic change. Expectations run high, and social and economic problems are pressing. As Iran enters the twentieth year of its Islamic revolution, the stabilization of the new regime seems to depend less on the degree of its return to Islam than on the degree to which it resolves the problems that initially fueled popular discontent.

Two decades after the revolution, the dispute over the appropriate path to advance the country has not yet been resolved.

The elections gave Khatami a mandate for change, but not the full authority to carry out his preferred policies, nor sufficient power to do so. The Iranian ship of state thus continues to drift from course to course, in its search for a proper equilibrium between dedication to its revolutionary convictions and the pressuring demands of governance, between religion and state, and between Islam and the West.

NOTES

1. For a detailed discussion of the events of 1997, including an analysis of the election campaign and results, see David Menashri, "Iran," in *Middle East Contemporary Survey 1997* 21 (Boulder, Colo: Westview, forthcoming).

2. "Nuri Impeachment Marks New 'Factional' Development," Islamic Republic News Agency (IRNA), June 11, 1998, quoting *Iran*, in FBIS-NES-98-162 (Foreign Broadcast Information Service–Near East and South Asia, online), June 12, 1998.

3. *Wall Street Journal*, May 26, 1997. See also, John Lancaster, "Khatemi: Iran's 'Ayatollah Gorbachev'; Election Winner Schooled in Islamic Revolution, Western Culture," *Washington Post*, May 25, 1997, p. A29.

4. *Al-Riyad* (Riyadh), June 8, 1997.

5. John Lancaster, "Iran's 'Ayatollah Gorbachev.'"

6. "Peaceful Evolutionist: Robin Allen on the Challenges Confronting Iran's President after His Landslide Victory," *Financial Times*, August 23, 1997, p. 7.

7. "IRNA—English Daily Refutes West's Expectations for Change," IRNA, August 5, 1997, quoting *Kayhan International,* in FBIS-NES-97-217, August 6, 1997.

8. John Lancaster, "Iranians Voted for New Ideas, Not a New System," *Washington Post*, May 26, 1997, p. A1.

9. "Khatami Election Address," Islamic Republic of Iran Broadcasting (IRIB-TV), May 10, 1997, in FBIS-NES-97-091, May 13, 1997.

10. "Paper Examines U.S. Motives for Holding Talks" (orignally in Persian: Hoseyn Saffar-Harandi, "What Does America Want?"),

Kayhan (Tehran), December 17, 1997, in FBIS-NES-97-352, December 20, 1997.

11. *Ettela'at*, December 12, 1989. Similarly in his interview in *Kayhan* (Tehran), December 11, 1989.

12. Patrick Clawson, *Business as Usual? Western Policy Options Toward Iran* (Washington, D.C.: American Jewish Congress, 1995), p. 12.

13. "Relations with U.S. Assessed," *Jahan-e Islam*, October 19, 1993, in FBIS-NES-DR-93-216, November 10, 1993, p. 52.

14. *Salam*, July 27, 1994.

15. "Majles Deputy on Culture Minister Designate," IRIB-TV, August 19, 1997, in FBIS-NES-97-232, August 21, 1997.

16. Shaul Bakhash, "Iran: The Crisis of Legitimacy," in *Middle Eastern Lectures* vol. 1 (Tel Aviv: Moshe Dayan Center, 1995), pp. 104, 109, 113–114.

17. Roy P. Mottahedeh, "The Islamic Movement: The Case of Democratic Inclusion," *Contention* 4, no. 3 (Spring 1995), p. 112.

18. "Nightmare Awaits Countries Misrepresenting Khatami Victory," *Iran News*, August 23, 1997, in FBIS-NES-97-235, August 26, 1997.

19. Shahram Chubin, *Iran's National Security Policy: Capabilities, Intentions, and Impact* (Washington, D.C.: Carnegie Endowment, 1994), pp. 65–68.

20. Robin Allen, "Peaceful Evolutionist."

21. David Menashri, *Iran: A Decade of War and Revolution* (New York: Holmes and Meier, 1990), pp. 83–84.

22. *Iran Weekly Press Digest* 10, no. 34 (August 16–22, 1997).

23. Bahman Baktiari and W. Scott Harrop, "Tables Turn on Iran's Islamic Extremists," *Christian Science Monitor*, April 16, 1996, p. 18.

24. Robin Allen, "Peaceful Evolutionist."

25. "IRNA—English Daily Refutes West's Expectations for Change," FBIS-NES-97-217.

26. *Kayhan International*, February 10, 1979.

27. "Khatami Speaks on Cabinet, Other Issues," IRIB-TV, August 13, 1997, in FBIS-NES-97-227, August 18, 1997.

28. *Ettela'at*, April 26, 1990. Responding, Mohtashami then wrote, that such a deviation from Khomeini's line was a "mistake that will never be forgiven," and condemned such views which, he said, "penetrated the body of the Islamic regime like a scourge"; *Kayhan* (Tehran), April 29, 1990. Yet, in 1997, Mohtashami supported Khatami, who appointed Mohajerani as minister.

29. *Salam*, April 15, 1996.

30. "Nuri Urges Diversity of Candidates in Majles Election," IRNA, January 24, 1996, in FBIS-NES-DR-96-018, January 26, 1996, pp. 49–50.

31. During the campaign, Khatami was often asked whether, if elected, he would appoint women ministers. His typical answer was: "In this regard, I make no distinction between men and women"; see as "Khatami on Cabinet Ministers, Women, Arts, Religion, Politics," *Iran*, March 16, 1997, in FBIS-NES-97-107, June 5, 1997.

32. In all previous governments (except Rafsanjani's 1989 cabinet) the Majlis rejected some of the proposed nominees. In June 1998 Nuri lost his cabinet post.

33. See more in his books and edited volumes of his lectures: Muhammad Khatami, *Zamine-haye Khizesh-e Mashruteh* (The Circumstances Behind the Emergence of Constitutionalism), (Tehran: Paya, n.d.); *Bim-e Mowj* (Fear of the Wave), (Tehran: Sima-ye Javan, 1993; second edition, 1995); *Az Donya-e 'Shahr' ta Shahr-e 'Donya'* (From the World of City to the City of the World), (Tehran: Nashr-e Ney, 1997); *Hope and Challenge: The Iranian President Speaks* (Binghamton: State University of New York, 1997); *Mutalla'at fi al-Din wal-Islam wal-'Asr* (Studies on Religion, Islam, and the Era), (Beirut: Dar al-Jadid, 1998).

34. See, for example, *Iran Times*, May 30, 1997.

35. *Jomhuri-ye Islami,* May 1, 1996, and *Kayhan* (Tehran), May 1, 1996.

36. *Ettela'at*, November 3, 1993.

37. "Majlis Speaker Says Defence of Palestinians 'Religious Obligations'," IRNA, February 7, 1997, in the BBC Summary of World

Broadcasts (BBC-SWB), February 8, 1997, p. 10.

38. "Complete Text of Khatami–Ardakani's Resignation," *Kayhan-e Hava'i*, July 29, 1992, in FBIS-NES-DR-92-165, August 25, 1992, pp. 50–52; see also: "Khatami Quit Because of 'Stagnant' Climate," Agence France Presse, July 18, 1992, in FBIS-NES-DR-92-139, July 20, 1992, pp. 68–69.

39. Laurent Lamote (pseudonym), "Domestic Politics and Strategic Intentions," in Patrick Clawson, ed., *Iran's Strategic Intentions and Capabilities* (Washington, D.C.: National Defense University, 1994), p. 12.

40. Khatami, *Mutala'at*, p. 21.

41. Khatami, *Bim-e Mowj*, p. 139.

42. Ibid., pp. 52, 172.

43. Khatami, *Hope and Challenge*, pp. 1, 19. See similarly his *Mutala'at*, mainly pp. 21–22; *Bim-e Mowj*, pp. 176–177.

44. Khatami, *Hope and Challenge*, pp. 1, 19; *Mutala'at,* pp. 21–22.

45. Khatami, *Az Donya-e Shahr*, pp. 14–15.

46. Khatami, *Mutala'at*, pp. 41–42, 79; Khatami, *Bim-e Mowj*, pp. 112, 176–177.

47. Khatami, *Bim-e Mowj*, pp. 185–191.

48. Khatami, *Mutala'at*, pp. 121, 139.

49. "Khatami Election Address," IRIB-TV, May 10, 1997, in FBIS-NES-97-091, May 13, 1997.

50. The decrees are cited in *Ettela'at*, January 7 and 12, 1988, and *Kayhan* (Tehran), January 7, 1988. See also, Menashri, *A Decade of War and Revolution*, pp. 386–387.

51. NHK Television (Tokyo), February 1, 1988, in BBC-SWB, February 3, 1988, pp. A4–A5. Also, Menashri, *A Decade of War and Revolution*, p. 387.

52. *Kayhan* (London), April 16, 1992.

53. "TV Roundtable with Election Candidates," IRIB-TV, May 20, 1997, in FBIS-NES-97-099, May 23, 1997.

54. "Khatami, Nateq Nuri on Satellite TV, Protecting Culture," IRIB-TV, May 19, 1997, in FBIS-NES-97-139, May 21, 1997.

55. "TV Roundtable with Election Candidates," FBIS-NES-97-099.

56. "Khatami Election Address," FBIS-NES-97-091.

57. "Paper Views Khatami Desire for Improved Ties with West" (editorial), *Iran News*, August 5, 1997, in FBIS-NES-97-222 August 12, 1997.

58. IRNA, December 9, 1997.

59. IRNA, December 14, 1997.

60. "IRNA Carries Khatami CNN Interview," IRNA, January 7, 1998, in FBIS-NES-98-007, January 11, 1998.

61. "Iran's Larijani Calls for Improved Relations With West," *Jomhuri-ye Islami*, November 13, 1997, in FBIS-NES-97-328, November 26, 1997.

62. "Iran's Kharrazi: 'Ball' in U.S. Court to Improve Relations," IRNA, December 23, 1997, in FBIS-NES-97-357, December 29, 1997.

63. See articles in *Salam* on January 27 and on February 2, 25, and 28, 1998.

64. See *Salam*, January 3 and February 2, 1998.

65. *Salam*, January 17, 1998.

66. "Iranian President: Quarrel with U.S. Government, Not Nation," IRIB-TV, November 4, 1997, in FBIS-NES-97-308, November 6, 1997.

67. See "IRNA Reports Khatami News Conference," IRNA, May 27, 1997, and "Further on Khatami's 27 May News Conference," IRIB-TV, May 27, 1997; both in FBIS-NES-97-102, May 29, 1997.

68. "Welcome Signal from Iran; Khatami's Conciliatory Tone at Islamic Conference Heartens West" (editorial), *Los Angeles Times*, December 11, 1997, p. B8.

69. IRNA, December 9, 1997.

70. *Kayhan* (Tehran), February 16, 1998. See also, "Iran News Reviews Press," *Iran News,* February 17, 1998, in FBIS-NES-98-054, February 26, 1998.

71. "Iran News: 'No Ties with U.S. Possible,'" *Iran News*, August 3, 1997, in FBIS-NES-97-220, August 12, 1997.

72. See, for example, articles in *Jomhur-ye Islami*, January 11, January 17, and February 2, 1998.

73. See articles in *Resalat*, January 11 and 17, 1998.

74. See articles in *Kayhan* (Tehran) on December 30, 1997, and on January 4, 8, 10, 11, and 17, 1998.

75. *Wall Street Journal*, May 26, 1997. Similarly, James Rubin cited in "Iranian Spokesman 'Responds' to U.S. Statement," IRNA, August 21, 1997, in FBIS-NES-97-233, August 22, 1997.

76. "Iranian Paper on Khatami Call for Dialogue with U.S.," IRNA, December 17, 1997, quoting *Kayhan International*, in FBIS-NES-97-351, December 19, 1997.

77. "Paper Examines U.S. Motives for Holding Talks" FBIS-NES-97-352.

78. *Jomhuri-ye Islami*, February 28, 1998.

79. Robert Snyder, "Explaining the Iranian Revolution's Hostility Toward the United States," *Journal of South Asian and Middle Eastern Studies* 17, no. 3 (Spring 1994), p. 19.

80. "Khatami Airs Views on Current Issues," IRIB-TV, May 27, 1997, in FBIS-NES-97-102, May 29, 1997; see also "Further on Khatami's 27 May News Conference," and "IRNA Reports Khatami News Conference," FBIS-NES-97-102.

81. IRNA, December 9, 1997.

82. IRNA, December 14, 1997.

83. "Khatami Condemns Zionist Attacks in Occupied Territories," IRIB-TV, September 1, 1997, in FBIS-NES-97-244, September 3, 1997.

84. "Khatami Speaks on Imam 'Ali's Anniversary," Tehran Television, January 19, 1998, in FBIS-NES-98-026, January 29, 1998.

85. *Tehran Times*, May 3, 1998. See also "Iran's Khatami Receives Shaykh Yasin," IRNA, May 2, 1998, in FBIS-NES-98-123, May 6, 1998.

86. IRNA, December 9, 1998.

87. "Iranian Paper on Khatami Call for Dialogue with U.S.," FBIS-NES-97-351.

88. "Iran News: 'No Ties with U.S. Possible,'" *Iran News*, August 3, 1997, in FBIS-NES-97-220, August 12, 1997.

89. See for example *Jomhuri-ye Islami*, April 7, 1998.

90. *Jomhuri-ye Islami*, October 4, 1997; see also the April 7, 1998, edition.

91. "Khamenei Tells Garaudy U.S. Completely Influenced by Zionism," IRNA, April 20, 1998, in FBIS-NES-98-110, April 21, 1998.

92. "Khamenei Receives Hamas Leader Yasin," IRIB-TV, May 2, 1998, in FBIS-NES-98-123, May 6, 1998.

93. See for example *Salam*, June 18, 1998.

94. "Iran News Views Press Comment on Karbaschi Trial," in FBIS-NES-163, June 15, 1998 (quoting *Rah-e Now*). See also *Kayhan International*, May 30, 1998; IRNA, "Iran's Khazali: Khatami Should Publicly Confess to Mistake," in FBIS-NES-98-148, June 1, 1998.

95. See for example, *Salam*, January 27, 1998. Such allusion, see also in *Kayhan* (Tehran), May 3, 1998, and in *Resalat*, May 3, 1998.

96. *Kayhan* (Tehran), May 28, 1998 and *Mobin*, May 2, 1998, brought as "Qom IRGC Commander's Remarks Against Khatami Criticized," FBIS-NES-98-125, May 8, 1998.

97. For his main charges, see David Menashri, *Revolution at a Crossroads: Iran's Domestic Politics and Regional Ambitions* (Washington, D.C.: The Washington Institute for Near East Policy, 1997), pp. 9–14. For a detailed discussion of the developments following Khatami's election see my chapter on Iran, *Middle East Contemporary Survey*, 1997.

98. *Resalat*, November 23, 1997.

99. *Kayhan* (London), December 4, 1997.

100. *Jomhuri-ye Islami* and *Kayhan* (Tehran), November 22, 1997.

101. *Jomhuri-ye Islami*, November 22; *Kayhan* (Tehran), November 23, 1997. See also, *Kayhan* (Tehran), December 27, 1997.

102. *Jomhuri-ye Islami*, November 22, 1997.

103. *Jomhuri-ye Islami*, November 27, 1997. See English translation in "Khamenei Speech on Recent 'Conspiracy,'" FBIS-NES-97-334,

December 7, 1997.

104. *Abrar*, November 22, 1997; *Jomhuri-ye Islami*, November 20, 1997.

105. *Jomhuri-ye Islami*, November 20, 1997.

106. *Jomhuri-ye Islami*, November 26, 1997.

107. *Resalat*, December 1, 1997; and "Worth Hearing: Stances of Engineer Bahonar," *Akhbar*, December 7, 1997, in FBIS-NES-97-343, Decemeber 17, 1997.

108. Menashri, *Revolution at a Crossroads*, pp. 17–19.

109. "Tehran Daily Views Iranian Reaction to Karbaschi Trial," *Kayhan International*, June 17, 1998, in FBIS-NES-98-174, June 25, 1998.

110. "IRNA Cites Judiciary Official on Karbaschi Arrest," IRNA, April 5, 1998, in FBIS-NES-98-095, April 7, 1998.

111. "Majles Deputy Rejects Karbaschi Arrest Political Move," IRNA, April 14, 1998, in FBIS-NES-98-104, April 16, 1998. Majlis member Morteza Nabavi argued that claiming that the detention of officials weakens the government, tantamount to providing them with immunity; see as "Majles Deputies Disagree on Karbaschi Arrest," IRNA, April 5, 1998, in FBIS-NES-98-095, April 7, 1998.

112. "Iranian Deputy: Karbaschi's Superiors 'Also Guilty'" (originally: Mehrdad Serjooie, "Rafsanjani Encouraged Karbaschi"), *Iran News*, June 13, 1998, in FBIS-NES-98-168, June 19, 1998.

113. "Tehran Daily Views Iranian Reaction to Karbaschi Trial," *Kayhan International*, June 17, 1998, in FBIS-NES-98-174, June 25, 1998.

114. "Majles Deputies Disagree on Karbaschi Arrest," FBIS-NES-98-095.

115. Ibid.

116. "Karbaschi Subject to Gruelling Interrogation," *Tehran Times*, April 9, 1998, in FBIS-NES-98-109, April 21, 1998.

117. "Interior Minister Visits Karbaschi's Family, Praises Mayor," IRNA, April 11, 1998, in FBIS-NES-98-101, April 15, 1998.

118. "Iranian Ministry to Form Karbaschi Defense Headquarters," IRNA, April 11, 1998, in FBIS-NES-98-101, April 15, 1998. Amir Kabir was the modernizer Qajar prime minister, assassinated in 1852.

119. "Ayatollah Taheri: Karbaschi Arrest 'Politically Motivated,'" *Hamshahri,* April 6, 1998, in FBIS-NES-98-104, April 16, 1998.

120. "Ayatollah Says Political Smell Attached to Karbaschi Issue," *Kar va Kargar,* April 7, 1998, in FBIS-NES-98-110, April 23, 1998.

121. "Interior Minister Attends Majles to Defend His Performance," IRNA, June 21, 1998, in FBIS-NES-98-172, June 23, 1998.

122. "Tehran Deputy—Nuri Impeachment Move Not Helpful to Unity," IRNA, June 17, 1998, in FBIS-NES-98-168, June 18, 1998.

123. "Iranian Daily: 'Nuri Was Fulfilling Promise of Freedom'" (originally in Persian: Kasra Nuri, "2nd Khordad to Be Impeached on Sunday"), *Salam,* June 18, 1998, in FBIS-NES-98-171, June 23, 1998.

124. "Iran Weekly—Impeachment of Nuri Attack Against Nation," *Mobin,* June 20, 1998, in FBIS-NES-98-176, June 29, 1998.

125. "Khatami: Government Will 'Definitely Make Good Use' of Nuri," IRNA, June 21, 1998, in FBIS-NES-98-172, June 23, 1998.

126. U.S. Department of State, Office of the Spokesman, Press Statement, June 17, 1998.

127. U.S. Department of State, Daily Press Briefing, June 18, 1998.

128. See, for example, Ayatollah Ahmad Janati, *Kayhan* (Tehran), May 30, 1998; articles in *Kayhan* (Tehran), May 30, June 14, and June 28, 1998; *Resalat,* May 30, 1998; *Farda,* June 14, 1998; and *Jomhuri-ye Islami,* May 28, 1998.

129. *Jomhuri-ye Islami,* June 20, 1998; *Resalat,* June 20 and June 27, 1998.

130. *Jame'e,* June 20 and June 27, 1998.

131. *Jame'e,* June 28, 1998. For harsh criticism of such statements see *Kayhan* (Tehran) and *Jomhuri-ye Islami,* July 1, 1998.

132. "Welcome Signal from Iran," *Los Angeles Times.*

Chapter 3

IRAN'S SICK ECONOMY
Prospects for Change under Khatami

Eliyahu Kanovsky

Muhammad Khatami's first year in office is too short a period for an assessment of his economic performance. Nevertheless, it can be said that little has happened to change Iran's serious economic problems. Since the 1979 Islamic revolution, "real incomes have sunk savagely, particularly for the disappearing middle class"; today, a teacher's pay barely covers the cost of renting a room.[1] Some four million exiles are abroad, a severe loss of talent from which Iran suffers to this day. In the manufacturing sector, much capacity lies idle.[2] One recent report on an aluminum company noted that only 9 percent of capacity was being utilized.[3] The state-owned industrial sector retains many unneeded workers, and there are many others underemployed, like those selling cigarettes in the streets.[4]

Although it would be unrealistic to expect Khatami to reverse these problems in only one year, it is legitimate to examine the fundamental economic problems facing Iran and then to see how Khatami's economic policies and his plan for economic reforms address those problems.

THE FUNDAMENTAL ECONOMIC PROBLEMS

Governance

Under the Islamic constitution the religious leader—not the elected president—controls the military, the judiciary, national security, intelligence, radio, and television; the president runs the economy and the government bureaucracy. But the religious leader can interfere and set broad policies, when he sees fit.[5] The existing system of governance makes it very difficult or impossible to institute far-reaching economic reforms; they can be blocked or emasculated by the religious authorities or by the Majlis (parliament). Economic reforms such as a realistic uniform exchange rate, privatization, or improving the tax system, among others, involve depriving certain people or groups of "easy money." Many of the latter are well-connected members of the religious and secular elite and can thwart the will of the president.

Indeed, a survey of the Iranian economy concludes, "economic mismanagement . . . and pervasive corruption hold back economic growth and investment."[6] Most of the wealth appropriated from Shah Mohammed Reza Pahlavi and his cronies was passed on to the new regime's cronies, "a new rich class just as greedy and corrupt as the old aristocrats."[7]

Stagnant Oil and Gas Industry

In a formal sense the oil sector in Iran accounted for about 17 percent of gross domestic product (GDP) in 1993–1996, but this figure is misleading. A far more meaningful assessment is oil's share of Iran's total exports—that is, foreign exchange earnings—which is around 80 percent. As one (unnamed) economist in Iran stated in early 1998, "Low oil prices are affecting everything and everyone."[8] Most of the economic sectors, industry in particular, are crucially dependent on oil export revenues to finance imports of production inputs and other goods.

During and after the revolution there was a sharp decline in oil production, apparently because of the flight of essential technicians, both foreign and Iranian. During the 1980–1988 war with Iraq, both countries were attempting to inflict maximum damage to the other's oil installations. Between 1973 and 1978—under the Shah—Iran's oil production had averaged 5.7 million barrels per day (bpd). At the end of hostilities in mid-1988, oil production was 2.3 million bpd. Production was raised to 3.6 million bpd by 1993 and remained at that level until 1997.[9]

The fact that Iranian output remained at the same level for five consecutive years was not a matter of deliberate policy. In the early 1990s, the Iranian oil minister announced plans to raise productive capacity to 4.5 million bpd by 1993.[10] That goal was not achieved. When OPEC decided on higher quotas for 1998, Iran was unable to raise production to its quota.[11] While in 1997, Venezuela, Nigeria, Libya, and other members of OPEC were exceeding their quotas. Iran was unable to follow suit, not because of any loyalty to OPEC, but because of its own constraints.[12]

The problem is not lack of oil. Iran's proven oil reserves are estimated to be 93 billion barrels, in the same league as Kuwait and the United Arab Emirates.[13] Rather, Iran apparently lacks a sufficient quantity of capital and skilled technicians to expand its productive capacity. As early as 1990, dire economic problems persuaded Iranian authorities to alter or ignore the revolutionary ideology that opposes the participation of foreign oil companies in the development of its oil and gas resources.

Iran has huge gas reserves, second only to Russia's. But geography and politics greatly restrict its ability to export gas. The big markets are in the United States, Western Europe, and the Far East, and transporting gas to these areas is hugely expensive. At a world gas conference in 1997, the Iranian oil minister announced ambitious plans for earnings of $3 billion per annum from gas exports by the year 2000, but he emphasized that without foreign investment these goals will not be realized.[14] The *Financial Times Survey of International Gas Industry* notes that both Qatar and Iran have huge reserves of natural gas and that during the last two years both have been trying to lure foreign investors into developing their natural gas resources. Qatar did so, with great success, but "thanks to its suffocating bureaucracy, and the threat of U.S. sanctions, [Iran] has little to show for its efforts."[15] The South Pars deal with the French firm Total is mainly for gas, but that will be used for domestic consumption initially; eventually, it may include gas shipments to Turkey.[16] The government in Tehran was able to finance on its own a gas pipeline linking Turkmenistan with Iran, which opened in December 1997, again providing gas for domestic consumption. Iran hopes eventually to serve as a conduit for exporting Turkmenistan gas to Turkey and possibly eventually to Western Europe.[17]

Meanwhile, Iran's domestic oil consumption has been rising rapidly. In large part this is because of enormous implicit subsidies—that is, because the government has been selling oil products domestically at ridiculously low prices as compared with international prices. From time to time the authorities raise domestic oil prices, but rapid inflation soon reduces the real price of oil products to very low levels. In addition to local consumption of the products of its own refineries, the government has had to allocate scarce foreign currency for imported oil products. In 1998 Iran allocated almost $1 billion in payment for imported refined oil products.[18] The very low prices of these products also encourage smuggling into neighboring countries. In effect, poor Iran is subsidizing—among others—some of its rich neighbors.

I have, for many years, argued that the longer-term fundamentals of the oil market point to low prices at least when measured in constant dollars.[19] That spells trouble for Iran. There are of course fluctuations—sometimes sharp fluctuations—in oil prices. In 1996, high prices were caused by unusual weather conditions in the northern hemisphere, as well as other factors. But that situation was reversed in late 1997, as oil prices came crashing down. Oil prices may recover from their low levels of early 1998, but sooner or later the fundamentals reassert themselves, and those are not favorable to high oil prices. Iran is ill-prepared for the current and future droughts in oil revenues.

Discouraging the Non-Oil Economy

Various Iranian ministers have announced grandiose plans for the rapid growth of non-oil exports. In mid-1997, just before President 'Ali Akbar Hashemi Rafsanjani left office, a master plan for the next twenty years was announced. According to the plan, oil revenues would remain stable at around $14 billion per annum, while non-oil exports would rise ten-fold to reach $48 billion by the year 2016, an average annual growth rate of 12.2 percent. According to the plan, the average annual growth rate of GDP would be an ambitious 7 percent, and, as a consequence, unemployment would drop to 5.2 percent (i.e., full employment would be achieved), or about one half the present unemployment rate, according to official estimates.

A 1992 study by Hashem Pesaran concludes that the system of multiple exchange rates introduced in the 1980s accounts for much of the poor performance of the Iranian non-oil economy.[20] The gap between the different official exchange rates, and between these and the black market rate, is so wide that there is a gross misallocation of resources and a very strong temptation for corruption. For many years the International Monetary Fund has pressed for a uniform and realistic exchange rate. Nevertheless, since 1995, the government has maintained a complex and constantly changing system of multiple exchange rates, including a rate of 1,750 rials to the dollar, used for favored imports (or favored importers); a rate of 3,000 rials to the dollar, used for other imports; a rate that in mid-1998 was 4,800 rials to the dollar, used for Iranians who want to travel abroad; and a free market rate that in mid-

1998 was about 5,500 rials to the dollar, used for some trans-actions.[21] Those who can persuade the authorities—and there are various ways of persuasion—to sell them dollars at the 1,750 rate becomes instant millionaires, because they can turn around and sell the dollars on the free market. The *bonyads* (religious foundations), the state-owned industries, and well-placed businesspeople receive preferential treatment in their purchases of foreign currency or their imports—in effect a huge hidden subsidy.

The system of multiple exchange rates also hurts export-ers and encourages imports instead of local products. Like its predecessors, the Khatami administration tries to compel businesspeople to accept a far smaller remuneration in rials for their dollars than is offered on the free market. As a result of tighter exchange rate rules and other adverse economic poli-cies, non-oil exports have actually fallen since 1995.[22] Carpet exports (dominated by the private sector) reached $2.13 bil-lion in 1994–1995. In the following year they were down by one half as a result of the new currency regulations. At the same time, the continued availability of dollars at the favored 1,750 rate allows imports to be cheaper than locally-made goods, which often have to use inputs imported at less favor-able exchange rates.

Macroeconomic Imbalances

In an article published in the spring of 1997, Jahangir Amuzegar spells out some of Iran's macroeconomics imbalances, includ-ing heavy external debt, double-digit inflation, and large cur-rent-account deficits.[23]

The government is unable to raise sufficient capital to reno-vate the country's aging infrastructure, in part because so many resources are devoted to subsidies. A very large hidden sub-sidy is the provision of oil products, electric power, and other utilities at very low prices. In March 1998, gasoline prices were the equivalent of less than sixty cents per U.S. gallon. Subsidies on energy—oil products, gas, and electricity—cost the economy about $11 billion annually.[24] Aside from the hidden subsidies (i.e., those not included in the budget), there are subsidies for food and essential services explicitly noted in the budget. In the 1998–1999 budget, $2.1 billion are designated as subsidies for basic goods. Moreover, the minister of commerce stated that this would not suffice.[25] In 1994, President Rafsanjani stated that the cost of subsidies, explicit plus implicit, was about $15 billion a year, a crushing burden considering that subsidies were equal to total oil export revenues that year.[26]

The large budgetary deficits are inflationary and the growth of the deficit adds more fuel to the inflationary fires. According to official estimates, inflation has been reduced in recent years from a peak of 50 percent in 1995 to 17 percent in 1997. Yet, "bankers familiar with Iran say that the real rate [of inflation] is probably double that."[27] The whole system of subsidies, direct and indirect, encourages consumption, waste, and corruption, rather than production efficiency and a more equitable distribution of income. Moreover. while in the short run subsidies and price controls may suppress some inflationary manifestations, the ensuing huge budgetary deficits increase inflationary pressures.

During President Rafsanjani's first term (1989–1993), Iran developed a serious foreign debt problem. Foreign debt was a low $6 billion when Rafsanjani assumed the presidency in 1989. While Khomeini, despite the war, shunned foreign borrowing (from a nationalist point of view), Rafsanjani engaged in large-scale borrowing, mainly short-term trade credits. Iran's external debt rose steeply to more than $23 billion in 1993. What was worse, since most of the debt was short-term, in 1993, Iran could not meet its debt obligations. Its creditors—largely Western European—rescheduled the debt to five- or six-year loans with payments to be completed around the year 2000.[28] To meet the debt obligations, the Iranian authorities have strongly limited imports and have used the positive current account balance to make payments on the debt. In 1990–1993, annual imports averaged $21.5 billion; in 1994–1997, they averaged $14.3 billion, a cutback of one third, causing severe problems for industry and other sectors.

INEFFICIENT AND OVERLY LARGE PUBLIC SECTOR

According to one estimate, the private sector accounts for only 14 percent of GDP. The remainder comes from a combination of the public sector (i.e., the government) and the bonyads, institutions unique to post-revolutionary Iran. Bonyads are special foundations set up by religious groups. They were given many of the shah's extensive properties and those belonging to his cronies. In some case these bonyads expanded to become powerful conglomerates. They do not publish budgets or other financial statements and are separate from the state-owned enterprises whose budgets are attached to the general budget of the treasury.

The bonyads control a large portion of the economy. The *Economist* estimates, "The biggest bonyad, the Foundation for the Deprived [*Bonyad-e Mostaz'afin*], has holdings of $12 billion, second only to the state-owned National Iranian Oil Company."[29] But as they have no shareholders and no public accounts and are answerable only to Iran's religious leader, the bonyads are a law unto themselves. They are supposed to use the profits from their enterprises to provide inexpensive housing, health care and other social services to the poor; in reality, much is siphoned off by those in control and relatively little reaches the needy.[30] According to the *Financial Times*, the bonyads have powerful influence, as they are

> directed by political appointees without regard to business experience. . .

Among the bonyads, the most notorious is the Bonyad-e Mostaz'afin, the "foundation for the oppressed and disabled." At its head is . . . a former minister of Iran's Revolutionary Guard Corps (IRGC), itself an industrial and defense conglomerate second in size only to the Mostaz'afin.

. . .Private businessmen and analysts say the number [working for the Mostaz'afin] is near 700,000, or some 5 percent of the male workforce.

Together with orthodox government ministries and nationalized industries, the Mostaz'afin and other state companies . . . have preferential access to scarce foreign exchange at rates reserved for favorites of the regime. They grant themselves industrial licenses and operate independently of government departments.

[One foundation] has its own bank which, unlike other . . . state banks, is exempt from keeping interest-free deposits [i.e., reserve requirements] with the central bank.

The autonomy of the bonyad is not confined to banking, commerce, or industry. One of them unilaterally took the initiative in 1989 to offer the $2 million "bounty" for Salman Rushdie. . .

. . .[Bonyads and state-owned companies] own or control all the country's twenty-one banks; transport companies; oil, petrochemical, and mining companies; and vast parts of the construction, manufacturing, and agricultural sectors.[31]

During the past few years the Iranian authorities appear to have become more and more convinced that without substantial foreign investment in oil, gas and petrochemicals, there is little or no prospect for any significant advance, let alone the realization of their ambition to have gas and petrochemicals, and other non-oil exports, substantially alter oil's position as the linchpin of their economy. Yet, U.S. sanctions are a serious deterrent to foreign investment. International companies think twice before taking actions that might jeopardize their relations with the United States, the world's economic superpower.

The Economic Dimensions of Security Expenditures

There is little hard information on the economic costs of Iran's military forces and adventures. According to estimates of the U.S. Arms Control and Disarmament Agency (ACDA), Iran's military expenditures as a ratio of gross national product (GNP) declined relatively steadily from 10.3 percent in 1986, the peak during the war with Iraq, to 2.6 percent in 1995. The ACDA reports that arms imports in the war years also peaked in 1986 at $2.6 billion and fell steadily thereafter to $270 million in 1995.

From time to time there are news reports of Iranian terrorist activities, including supporting Hizballah in Lebanon; the bombing of the Israeli embassy in Argentina in 1992; and the bombing of the Buenos Aires Jewish community center in 1994.[32] There are reports of major arms purchases and the building of a nuclear reactor with Russian technical aid. There are reports of Iran building a new missile with a range of about 800 miles, long enough to reach Israel and, of course, Saudi Arabia and other Gulf countries.[33] The sanctions that the United States has imposed on investments in Iran's oil and gas industry are based on the U.S. government's assessment that these reports are reasonably accurate.

On the other hand, the wide range of military and terrorist activities and the large number of Iranians in the armed forces (both regular and irregular) casts doubt on the ACDA estimates that military expenditures absorbed only 2.6 percent of Iran's GNP in 1995.[34] It is not uncommon for many countries to hide part of their military expenditures under other headings in the budget or for these expenditures to be outside the budget. Moreover, in the case of Iran it appears that the bonyads may be an important source of funding for these activities, including supporting the revolutionary guards. The bonyads' budgets are not published and, as previously mentioned, the foundations themselves are accountable to no one, including the president and his ministers, other than to the religious leader, Ayatollah 'Ali Khamene'i.

KHATAMI'S ECONOMIC POLICIES

Khatami faces an unfavorable external economic situation. Since 1997, oil prices have been considerably lower, which adds enormously to Iran's problems. Oil export revenues fell sharply from $19.3 billion in 1996 to $16.2 billion in 1997,[35] and 1998 looks even worse; revenues could be as low as $12 billion.[36] Projections for 1999 are for continued hardship. The problem of government budget deficits becomes far more acute when oil revenues decline. The new finance minister under Khatami disclosed that in 1997–1998 there would be a very large budgetary deficit of about $5 billion. His predecessor had claimed that the budget was in balance.[37] As for 1998–1999, the government had originally assumed an oil price of $17.50 a barrel. The Majlis, in its revisions of the budget assumed that the price would be $16. In April 1998 the government again revised the 1998–1999 budget, assuming a price of $12. The president stated that the drop in oil prices would create an additional shortfall in the budget of $4 billion.[38] This situation calls for a dramatic policy response which was not forthcoming as of mid-1998.

It is true that Khatami has been openly critical of the economic situation, calling the economy "sick."[39] In mid-1998, he said that the government is studying "structural changes."[40] On the first anniversary of his inauguration (August 2, 1998), he presented his much anticipated economic program. While acknowledging the economy was "chronically ill," he proposed few measures to resolve the problems he detailed; instead, he defended existing inefficient programs, like massive subsidies on gasoline, arguing "social equity has priority over production growth" (even though most of the subsidy's benefits go to the middle class not the poor).[41] To date, he has done little to address the fundamental problems identified above, except in the area of attracting foreign investment in oil and gas:

- Governance: He criticizes large-scale tax evasion and privilege-grabbing by the rich. At the same time, he has not abolished rules such as the system of multiple exchange rates, which is a major source of enrichment of the few at the expense of the state.

- Stagnant oil and gas industry: The Khatami government appears to have gone further than its predecessor by opening nearly all aspects of oil and gas development, onshore as well as offshore, to foreign investors. This includes exploration, development, and enhanced recovery.[42] Yet, there are few takers.[43] Either international oil companies, now welcomed and even sought after in many third world countries, find the prospects for profits better elsewhere, or they fear U.S. sanctions, or both. The chief executive of British Petroleum stated candidly in March 1998 that his company was looking carefully at possible investments in Iran's oil and gas sector and petrochemicals but that it was holding back until the issue of U.S. sanctions against non-American companies doing business with Iran and Libya is clarified—that is, removed.[44] The biggest success of the Khatami government in attracting foreign oil and gas investment came in the South Pars field, with a consortium involving the French firm Total and a Russian and a Malaysian firm. In May 1998, President Clinton waived sanctions against these companies.[45]

- Discouraging the non-oil economy: Khatami calls for boosting non-oil exports, but no measures have been taken in that direction. He calls on the wealthy to invest in Iran and to be satisfied with a "just" profit; presumably he was referring to the many Iranians who fled with their capital during and since the 1979 revolution. Yet,

Khatami has denounced the unjust profits and tax evasion of the rich, which is not likely to help in attracting the funds back to Iran.

- Macroeconomic imbalances: Khatami has taken only limited steps to contain the mushrooming 1998 budget deficit, hit hard by the fall in oil prices. At the same time, he told the Iranian people that his government would continue to subsidize basic foodstuffs and would not cut its welfare programs. His government's strategy for combating rising inflation has been to enforce strict price controls. The president told an official group charged with enforcing controls that price increases were the work of a "handful of opportunist elements," and he ordered the supervisors to "severely confront economic saboteurs."[46]

- Inefficient and overly large public sector: He calls for cutting down the state sector—that is, he favors privatization—and also calls for reducing state monopolies. Again, the president's goals may be laudable, but there is no apparent follow-up in terms of implementation.

- The economic dimensions of security expenditures: There is no indication that he has reduced military spending.

In short, the Khatami government faces serious economic challenges, both in the short term and in the long run, and it has taken modest steps at best.

CONCLUSIONS

Iran has a far more diversified economy than its neighbors in the Gulf. But it is as oil-dependent as they are, because of Iran's failure to improve and expand agriculture and industry, in particular, and its inability to make them important sources of export revenues. The Iranian economy inherited by President Khatami is, as he phrased it, a "sick economy." Basic economic reforms face numerous obstacles. As a rule, the

Various Economic Indicators—Iran

	1989[1]	1990	1991	1992	1993	1994	1995	1996	1997
Change in GDP[2] (percent)	3.3	11.7	11.4	5.7	1.6	0.7	4.2	4.7	3.2
Change in Consumption[3] (percent)	-1.1	21.2	12.4	3.5	3.4	6.0	1.1	2.3	N/A
Oil Production (in millions of bpd)	2.9	3.3	3.4	3.5	3.6	3.6	3.6	3.6	3.6
Oil Exports[4] (in $ billions)	12.0	17.9	16.0	16.9	14.3	14.6	15.1	19.3	16.2
Other Exports[4] (in $ billions)	1.0	1.3	2.6	3.0	3.7	4.8	3.3	3.2	3.7
Imports[4] (in $ billions)	13.4	18.3	25.2	23.3	19.3	12.6	12.8	15.0	16.7
Current account balance[5] (in $ billions)	-0.2	0.3	-9.5	-6.5	-4.2	5.0	3.4	5.2	1.0
External Debt (in $ billions)	6.0	9.0	11.3	16.0	23.4	22.7	21.9	16.8	11.6
Oil Price[6] ($ per barrel)	17.2	22.0	18.3	18.2	16.8	15.9	17.2	20.4	19.2
Inflation[7] (percent)	22.3	7.6	17.1	25.6	21.2	31.5	49.6	28.9	17.2
Military Expenditure to GNP[8] (Ratio)	6.4	6.0	5.1	3.0	3.4	3.5	2.6	N/A	N/A
Arms Imports[8] (in $ billions)	1.8	1.9	1.6	0.8	1.1	0.4	0.3	N/A	N/A

Sources: Central Bank of the Islamic Republic of Iran, *Economic Report* (Annual); Central Bank of the Islamic Republic of Iran, *Bulletin* (Quarterly); Central Bank of the Islamic Republic of Iran, *Economic Trends* (Quarterly); International Monetary Fund, *International Financial Statistics* (Monthly and Annual); Economist Intelligence Unit, *Country Report: Iran* (Quarterly and Annual)

greater the distortions, the greater the pain inflicted by economic reforms, and in Iran the distortions are unusually large. But what compounds the problem is the system of governance. The president, who is constitutionally charged with dealing with economic affairs, is hampered by the lack of sufficient authority to make basic changes. Thus far he has not announced any basic reforms. Compounding the problems are the U.S. sanctions which hamper development in the oil, gas, and petrochemical industries. Unless Iran finds a political formula for basic economic reforms, its economy will continue to flounder and stagnate. Political and social problems are the almost inevitable consequence.

Notes on Economic Table

1. Most of the official data is based on the calendar used in Iran. Fiscal year 1989 in the table begins on March 21, 1989 and ends on March 20 1990, and so forth.

2. Change in GDP (gross domestic product) refers to the percentage change from the previous year in real terms—that is, corrected for inflation.

3. The change in consumption refers to private consumption in real terms—that is, corrected for inflation

4. The data for the external accounts are in billions of dollars. Other exports refer to non-oil goods exports. The figures for imports refer to imports of goods, not services. Export and import figures are FOB (free on board).

5. The current account balance refers to exports of goods and services, minus the imports of goods and services, plus or minus unilateral transfers depending on whether they are receipts or payments of transfers.

6. The oil price figures are annual averages of the "average" price of a barrel of oil. These are reported by the International Monetary Fund.

7. The inflation figures refer to annual percentage changes in the cost of living index.

8. The figures for military expenditures and arms imports are from the U.S. Arms Control and Disarmament Agency *World Military Expenditures and Arms Transfers 1996* (Washington, D.C.: ACDA, July 1997), and earlier editions; the ratio is to gross national product (GNP) rather than to gross domestic product (GDP).

CHAPTER NOTES

1. "The Mullahs' Balance-Sheet," *Economist*, January 18, 1997, p. S4.

2. "Hard Times: How Not to Attract Investment," *Economist*, January 18, 1997, p. S14.

3. "Iran in Brief," *Middle East Economic Digest* (*MEED*), May 8, 1998, p. 23.

4. Economist Intelligence Unit (EIU), *Country Profile: Iran 1996/ 97*, (London: EIU, 1997), p. 14.

5. Elaine Sciolino, "Duelling Mullahs: Iran's Gladhander Takes On the Leader," *New York Times*, March 29, 1998, p. A4.

6. "The Mullahs' Balance-Sheet,"p. S3.

7. Ibid., p. S4.

8. Robin Allen, "Fear of Oil Price Fall Starts to Haunt Gulf Producers," *Financial Times*, January 28, 1998, p. 5.

9. See accompanying table.

10. *Mideast Markets*, November 1991, p. 33.

11. Bhushan Bahree, "Saudis Offer Tough Terms to Help Solve Oil Glut," *Wall Street Journal*, February 19, 1998, p. A2.

12. *Petroleum Economist* (London), December 1997, p. 4.

13. British Petroleum, *BP Statistical Review of World Energy, June 1998* (London: BP, 1998), p. 4.

14. *Petroleum Economist World Gas Conference 1998* (London: 1998).

15. Robert Allen, "Lost Opportunities as Politics Hinder Prosperity,"

Financial Times, June 10, 1997, p. 4.

16. Robert Corzine, "Caspian Coup for Iran as Turkmen Pipeline Opens," *Financial Times*, December 30, 1997, p. 1.

17. Ibid.

18. *Petroleum Intelligence Weekly* (PIW), February 1998, p. 2.

19. Eliyahu Kanovsky, *The Economic Consequences of the Persian Gulf War: Accelerating OPEC's Demise*, Policy Paper no. 30 (Washington, D.C.: The Washington Institute for Near East Policy, 1992).

20. M. Hashem Pesaran, "The Iranian Foreign Exchange Policy and the Black Market for Dollars," *International Journal of Middle East Studies* (February 1992), pp. 101–121.

21. EIU, *Country Profile: Iran 1997/98*, p. 40; "Government Faces Bread Price Criticism," *MEED* May 8, 1998, p. 22.

22. See accompanying table.

23. Jahangir Amuzegar, "Iran's Economy and U.S. Sanctions," *Middle East Journal* (Spring 1997), pp. 197–198.

24. Vahe Petrossian, "Now for the Hard Part," *MEED*, March 13, 1998, p. 3.

25. "Government Faces Bread Price Criticism," *MEED*, May 8, 1998, p. 22.

26. EIU, *Country Report: Iran*, Second Quarter 1994, p. 17.

27. *Middle East Economic Survey (MEES)*, April 20, 1998, p. B1.

28. EIU, *Country Profile: Iran 1997/98*, pp. 53–55.

29. "Dual Control: So Many Ways of Pulling Strings," *Economist*, January 18, 1997, p. S7.

30. "For the Oppressed," *Economist*, September 25, 1993, p. 54.

31. Robin Allen, "State Foundations Dominate Economy," *Financial Times*, July 17, 1997, p. 4.

32. Clifford Krauss, "Argentina Arrests 8 Iranians and Ousts 7 in Anti-Jewish Bombings," *New York Times*, May 17, 1998, p 15.

33. Michael R. Gordon, "Nuclear Fallout: A Whole New World of Arms Races to Contain," *New York Times*, May 3, 1998, p. D1.

34. See accompanying table.

35. See accompanying table.

36. *MEES*, April 27, 1998, p. B1.

37. "Ministries Told to Keep Spending Low," *MEED*, September 26, 1997, p. 12.

38. "Revised Budget Fixes Oil at $12 a Barrel," *MEED*, May 1, 1998, p. 19.

39. "Oil and Gas Projects Opened Up to Foreign Investors," *MEED*, March 27, 1998, p. 21.

40. "Khatami Presents Economic Recovery Plan," *Islamic Republic of Iran* Broadcasting, August 2, 1998, in FBIS-NES-98-218 (Foreign Broadcast Information Service–Near East and South Asia, online), August 6, 1998.

41. AFP, "Khatami Unveils Policies to Heal Iran's Economy," Internet, August 2, 1998; and "Khatami Pledges Economic Reform," *Financial Times,* August 3, 1998, p. 4 (no author given).

42. "Oil and Gas Projects Opened Up to Foreign Investors," *MEED*.

43. *PIW*, August 18, 1997, p. 2.

44. Robert Corzine, "BP Ready to Invest in Iran if US Line Eases," *Financial Times*, May 6, 1998, p. 4.

45. "What to Do About Iran," *Economist*, May 23, 1998, p. 41.

46. "Price Rises Prompt Crackdown," *MEED*, May 1, 1998, p. 19.

Chapter 4

THE MILITARY DIMENSION

Michael Eisenstadt

The May 1997 election of Muhammad Khatami as president of Iran has raised hopes and expectations of change in Iran's domestic and foreign policy. In the foreign policy arena, it is possible to discern a new vocabulary emphasizing "détente," "stability," and a "dialogue between civilizations," as well as efforts to defuse tensions with former adversaries. The latter includes a diplomatic "charm offensive" to mend fences with Iran's Gulf neighbors—most notably Saudi Arabia (though in fact the rapprochement between Tehran and Riyadh antedates Khatami's election)—and an opening to the American people in Khatami's January 1998 CNN interview.

Iran's defense and foreign policies, however, show more continuity than change. Whereas Iran's conventional military buildup seems to have run out of steam—at least for now—its policy regarding weapons of mass destruction (WMD) has been characterized by near total continuity. Iran continues to expand its arsenal of missiles and its civilian nuclear program—which most analysts believe is intended to serve as the foundation for a nuclear weapons program. Iran likewise continues to support groups that engage in terrorism and continues its attacks on oppositionists—though, it seems, at a reduced pace. Finally, Iran remains unremittingly hostile toward Israel, although it is possible to discern perhaps the first faint signs of change with regard to Iran's approach to the Arab–Israeli conflict. The one area of potentially dramatic change, however, is in the realm of political–military relations.

POLITICAL–MILITARY RELATIONS

Following the inauguration of President Khatami in August 1997, the Iranian government undertook perhaps the most far-reaching shake-up of the top levels of the military and security apparatus since the early days of the Islamic Republic. Nearly every key position changed hands, including the ministers of defense, intelligence, and interior; commanders of the Islamic Revolutionary Guard Corps (IRGC) and the Basij militia; and commanders of the regular army, the regular and IRGC naval arms, and the IRGC air force.[1] These changes were part of the general turnover of government positions— both civilian and military—that accompanied the formation of the new government in August–September 1997. Supreme Leader 'Ali Khamene'i, as commander-in-chief of the armed forces, is responsible for military appointments, and he probably agreed to this shake-up to meet popular demand for change while attempting to preserve continuity in policy.[2] For Khatami, this was an opportunity to demonstrate his ability to follow through on promises of change and to consolidate his position by flushing out hardline conservative opponents in key security, defense, and foreign policy billets.

Many of the new appointees were largely unknown outside of Iran, which makes it difficult to assess the background or potential political implications of these changes. Three of the changes, however, were clearly significant. 'Ali Shamkhani, the new minister of defense, was generally considered to represent those officers in the IRGC who wanted the organization to evolve into a more professional, apolitical institution.[3] In his first public address after his appointment, Shamkhani announced that "détente" in the Persian Gulf would be the highest priority of his ministry.[4] Moreover, former Intelligence Minister 'Ali Fallahian had opposed Khatami's candidacy and was considered one of the personalities most deeply implicated in Iran's past terrorist activities. He was replaced by a Majlis (parliament) deputy, Qorbanali Dorri Najafabadi, who had supported Khatami's candidacy and had no background in intelligence matters. Finally, the resignation of IRGC commander Mohsen Reza'i, after serving in this position for sixteen years, was a major milestone; his successor, however— former deputy IRGC commander Yahya Rahim Safavi—was believed to share his hardline views.

This became clear in May 1998, when Safavi reportedly made a number of harsh comments about the policies of President Khatami and his government to a gathering of IRGC commanders, which were subsequently leaked to the Iranian press. In his comments, Safavi reportedly berated Minister of Culture 'Ata'ollah Mohajerani for allowing the emergence of scores of new newspapers, many of which had been critical of the dominant conservative clerical faction, and he upbraided Interior Minister Abdollah Nuri for failing to quell student unrest in Tehran and strikes in Najafabad protesting the house arrest of Ayatollah Hossein 'Ali Montazeri, who had criticized Khamene'i and the system of clerical rule. Safavi bitterly complained that "Liberals . . . have taken over our universities, and our youth are now shouting slogans against despotism. We are seeking to root out counter-revolutionaries wherever they are. We have to behead some and cut off the tongues of others. Our language is our sword. We will expose these cowards."[5]

Safavi's comments flew in the face of Khatami's September 1997 warning to the IRGC to stay out of politics, and they raised the prospect of a more assertive political role for the Revolutionary Guard and the potential for greater conflict between conservatives (led by Khamene'i and by Majlis speaker 'Ali Akbar Nateq Nuri) and their reformist opponents (led by Khatami).[6] Yet, if reports that guard personnel voted for Khatami in the same proportion as the general population (69 percent) are true, it is not clear that hardline IRGC commanders could actually deliver their troops in the event of a showdown.[7]

Thus, for instance, if the president's conservative opponents were to press Khamene'i for Khatami's dismissal (as is permitted by the constitution)—an act that would probably spark widespread riots and demonstrations—it is possible that many IRGC and Basij militia troops would refuse orders to quell the unrest. This would leave the regime dependent on the thugs of the Ansar-e Hezbollah to do the job.[8] Although these people might be able to intimidate the enemies of the hardline conservatives, there are too few of them and they are not sufficiently well-organized to deal with widespread popular violence.[9]

CONVENTIONAL FORCES

Iran's conventional weapons procurement effort seems to have run out of steam in the past year or so.[10] This is not because Iran no longer feels the need to expand and to modernize its conventional forces, but apparently because it believes that, given its current financial constraints (in large part owing to the dramatic decline in world oil prices in the past year), available funds are best spent augmenting its WMD and missile-delivery capabilities. Moreover, Iran's domestic arms production efforts appear to have finally reached a take-off point, and what limited resources are available for conventional arms procurement are apparently being pumped into this area.[11]

For instance, in the past year, Iran has unveiled a number of new locally produced weapons systems. Whereas in the past Iran has often made exaggerated claims about its domestic military–industrial prowess, there is reason to believe that there is now some truth to the pronouncements, as it has produced photos of assembly lines and finished systems to back up its claims. Iran unveiled prototypes of the Thunder-1 and -2 self-propelled guns, the *Tosan* (Fury) light tank, and BMT-2 and Cobra armored personnel carriers (APCs); it announced that production of the propeller-driven *Parastu* (Swallow) and jet-powered *Dorna* (Lark) training aircraft would commence shortly; and it stated that mass production of the Boraq APC and the Zulfiqar main battle tank had begun.[12]

Iran has also continued with its highly active schedule of naval exercises in the Persian Gulf. Yet, contrary to past practice—when it used naval maneuvers as a form of muscle-flexing directed against its Gulf neighbors—Iran has, during the past year, tried to put a benign face on these exercises. For instance, during Victory-8 naval exercises in October 1997, regular Iranian Navy commander Abbas Mohtaj and IRGC Navy commander 'Ali Akbar Ahmadian stressed that the goal of the exercise was "peace, friendship, and stability."[13] Iranian commanders also introduced a new propaganda theme: They alleged that the use of depleted uranium ammunition by U.S. ships during maneuvers and the presence of chemical, biological, and nuclear weapons on board ships of the U.S. Fifth Fleet contributed to the pollution of the Persian Gulf. By contrast, Iranian commanders stated that they would use blank training rounds during naval maneuvers and shorten the duration of those exercises so as not to harm the marine environment in the Gulf, and to cultivate the image of Iran as a good neighbor.[14]

Iranian naval vessels also, for the first time, conducted port calls in Saudi Arabia (the support ship Kharg visited the port of Jiddah in March 1998), and Iran and Kuwait reportedly are considering joint naval exercises, further highlighting Iranian efforts to reduce tensions in the region.[15] This would be the first joint military exercise between Iran and one of its Arab neighbors since the 1979 revolution (Iran held its first joint military exercise since the revolution with Pakistan in 1994, and another exercise with Pakistan is reportedly planned for the near future). The goals of such moves, according to Defense Minister Shamkhani, are to "start with visits by vessels, appointing observers for exercises and using each other's training centers, and eventually carrying out joint exercises and, step-by-step, reaching the more sensitive stages of security cooperation."[16] Such a tack marks a dramatic departure from Iran's past approach toward its Arab neighbors. Whereas these gestures probably do not mean that Iran has abandoned the use of threats as an instrument of foreign policy, it would seem to indicate that some in Iran recognize that the frequent resort to intimidation in the past was counterproductive and drove the other Gulf states into the embrace of the United States. They realize that Iran can probably better achieve its goal of forging regional security arrangements that will make the U.S. presence superfluous through confidence-building measures and a policy of good-neighborliness toward the Gulf states. It remains to be seen whether Iran can succeed in convincing its skeptical Arab neighbors that it is no longer a threat.

In early 1998, the Iranian navy also found itself playing a key role in that country's complex relationship with Iraq and the United States. Since 1993, the Iranian navy had cooperated in the smuggling of Iraqi oil in violation of United Nations (UN) sanctions. Typically, Iraqi boats laden with oil would depart Basra and link up near the Shatt al-'Arab with IRGC naval units that would check the ship's documentation and collect a commission fee. The smugglers would then head east along Iran's coastline, remaining within Iranian territorial waters until approaching the Strait of Hormuz. From there, they would dash south to Dubai in the United Arab Emirates, assisted by lookouts in dinghies assisting the contraband runners in avoiding the multinational Maritime Interdiction Force that enforces sanctions on Iraq. Yet, in January 1998, at the height of the U.S. standoff with Iraq over the latter's obstruction of UN weapons inspections, the Iranian navy started cutting back its cooperation with smugglers—possibly as a conciliatory gesture to the United States. Smuggling declined dramatically in March and April but started increasing again by May, and some speculated that the increase was because of Iranian disappointment with America's failure to reciprocate this and other friendly gestures.[17]

Finally, whereas Iraq and the Persian Gulf region were the main foci of Iran's defense and foreign policies in the decade following the end of the Iran–Iraq War, developments in Afghanistan have increasingly held the attention of Iran's civilian and military leadership in the year since Khatami's inauguration. Iran has long been indirectly involved in the protracted internal struggle in Afghanistan that followed the Soviet withdrawal in 1989, supporting the Northern Alliance—nominally headed by Burhanuddin Rabbani—with arms and other forms of assistance. Iran fears that the Pakistani-supported Taliban government in Afghanistan could stir unrest among the two million Afghans in Iran, who provide much manual labor in large cities, and could contribute to heightened Sunni–Shi'i tensions in eastern Iran, where the Sunni minority constitutes one-third of the population. In addition, some Iranians suspect that a series of attacks by the opposition Mojahedin-e Khalq organization in 1998—including the June bombing of a courthouse in Tehran, the assassination of the former head of the Evin Prison Assadollah Ladjeverdi in August, and the attempted assassination of the head of the Foundation of the Oppressed Mohsen Rafiqdust in September—may have originated from Afghanistan.

The Northern Alliance suffered a series of setbacks in 1998 at the hands of its Taliban rivals, and by August 1998 it was in full retreat, with the Taliban controlling nearly all of Afghanistan. On top of these setbacks, eight Iranian diplomats and a journalist (along with thousands of Shi'i Hazara Afghans) were executed by members of the Taliban militia in August 1998 after the fall of the town of Mazar-e Sharif, leading to calls for vengeance in Iran and a military buildup on the Afghani border by Iranian forces later that month.[18] Tehran had several options: allow Afghan refugees armed and trained by Iran to cross the border to fight the Taliban; seize the northwestern part of Afghanistan around Herat to create a safehaven from which Iranian-armed Afghan guerillas might operate; or launch limited retaliatory air strikes on the Taliban. In response to the buildup, a Taliban spokesman warned that his organization "will target Iranian cities" if Afghanistan is attacked.[19] Although it remains unclear how this crisis will be resolved, the Taliban victory in Afghanistan introduces a new factor into Iran's security calculus that could complicate Iranian national security planning for years to come.

WEAPONS OF MASS DESTRUCTION

Iran continues to devote significant resources to its WMD programs. Most notably, it has continued with efforts to build up its strategic missile forces and it continues efforts to expand its civilian nuclear infrastructure, which it probably intends to use as a stepping stone to a nuclear weapons program.

Iran has been trying since the mid-1980s to acquire a missile production capability so it could end its reliance on external supply sources. This effort was plagued by various bottlenecks, including a shortage of skilled personnel, special materials, technological expertise, and adequate financing. As a result, until recently, Iran had little success in creating an indigenous missile production capability.[20]

This may be changing, however, thanks to aid provided by Russia, China, and North Korea during the past three to four years. This assistance includes equipment, machinery, components (including guidance systems), and special materials required to produce missiles. At present, Iran can produce Scud missiles domestically,[21] and it is reportedly building two liquid-fuel systems with substantial help from Russia: The Shehab-3, based on the North Korean Nodong-1, is expected to have a range of 1,300 kilometers (km), and the Shehab-4, based on Soviet SS-4 and/or North Korean Taepo-Dong technology, is expected to have a range of 2,000 km. (Iran reportedly even has plans for a follow-on missile with an intercontinental range.) In 1997, Iran conducted between six and eight static ground tests of the motor for the Shehab-3, and in July 1998 it conducted a test launch of the Shehab-3 that ended with the explosion of the missile in a fireball less than two minutes after launch.

Acquiring the ability to produce Scud-B or -C missiles with ranges of 300 km to 500 km proved a long and difficult process for Iran. Producing a missile such as the Shehab-3 or -4 capable of traveling 1,300 km to 2,000 km is an even more difficult proposition. These greater ranges translate to greater initial and terminal velocities, a higher flight trajectory, more prolonged stress on the missile airframe, and greater problems with heat buildup. This requires a more sturdy airframe, a more accurate guidance system, and the widespread use of exotic materials that can withstand high temperatures and stress—materials available from only a limited number of sources. It is not clear that North Korea has overcome all these technical and technological challenges—hence the importance of Russian assistance to Iran's medium-range missile programs.[22]

The United States has engaged in strenuous efforts to stanch the flow of missile technology and know-how from Russia to Iran in the past two to three years through a series of high-level meetings, though it is not clear yet how successful these efforts have been or whether it is too late for them to have a significant effect on Iranian activities in this area. According to leaked intelligence estimates, the Shehab-4 is likely to make its first test flight within two to five years.[23] Iran is also believed to be building a short-range solid-fuel missile known as the NP-110 (with a range of about 150 km) with Chinese help.[24]

The eventual deployment of the Shehab-3 will raise regional tensions, though it will not transform the regional balance of power. Syria's deployment of SS-21 missiles in 1983 and the deployment of al-Husayn missiles in western Iraq in 1989 led to heightened tensions with Israel and speculation about the possibility of Israeli preventive strikes against missile launch sites in Syria and Iraq. Iran's deployment of missiles capable of reaching Israel is likely to usher in a similar period of heightened regional tension, though it is also worth remembering that the earlier episodes passed without a confrontation.

The Shehab-3 (and subsequently the Shehab-4) will provide Iran with a variety of new capabilities. American missile defenses could have problems intercepting Shehab-3s flying either depressed (low-level) or lofted (high-altitude) trajectories against targets in the Gulf region. Moreover, the Shehab-3 will enable Iran to target Israel, Turkey, and Egypt directly. Thus, the knowledge that they are within range of Iranian missiles could influence decisions by Cairo and Ankara during an Iranian–U.S. crisis—however unlikely that might now be— and constrain U.S. military options. Likewise, the Shehab-4 will be capable of flying depressed or lofted trajectories against Israel, Turkey, and Egypt, complicating the defenses of these countries by presenting a more difficult target for American or Israeli antimissile defenses. The Shehab-4 will also be able to reach southern Europe by following a maximum-range medium-level trajectory. In any case, the longer ranges of the Shehab-3 and -4 will enable Iran to launch its missiles from deep within the interior of the country, complicating efforts to find and destroy missile launchers and crews.

Iran's known nuclear technology base is at present rather

rudimentary, though it is building an extensive civilian nuclear infrastructure that could serve as a springboard for a weapons program. In particular, its apparent investigation of various enrichment techniques (gas centrifuge enrichment in particular), its efforts to acquire nuclear research reactors and power plants, and reports of Iranian efforts to obtain fissile material in the former Soviet Union have raised questions about Iran's intentions.

Iran's strategy seems to be to build up its civilian nuclear infrastructure while avoiding activities that would clearly violate its Nuclear Non-Proliferation Treaty (NPT) commitments, using its new contacts in Russia and China to gain experience, expertise, and dual-use technology that could assist in creating a military program. Tehran could probably acquire a nuclear capability within a few years if it were to obtain fissile material and help from abroad; without such help, it could take Iran ten years or more to do so. The acquisition of research reactors, power plants, and nuclear technology from Russia and China would ultimately aid Iran's efforts. Without such outside help, Iran would probably face formidable obstacles to realizing its nuclear ambitions.[25] In fact, developments during the past year show that Iran's civilian nuclear program does face a number of obstacles, but that it is continuing efforts to acquire nuclear fuel cycle–related technologies from abroad.

Shortly after President Khatami's inauguration in August 1997, he appointed Oil Minister Gholamreza Aghazadeh to head the Atomic Energy Organization of Iran (AEOI). Aghazadeh's predecessor, Reza Amrollahi, was widely regarded as incompetent, and some observers feared that Aghazadeh—generally regarded as a competent administrator at the oil ministry—might revitalize the effort. Upon taking his new job, Aghazadeh announced that he intended to continue Iran's civilian nuclear program with the purchase of several new reactors, following the completion of the one currently under construction at Bushehr. (This new order reportedly would include two 300-MWe [megawatt-electric] units from China, possibly to be located at Darkhovin, and two 440-MWe units and another 1,000-MWe unit from Russia, to be located at Bushehr.)[26]

Bushehr, however, continues to experience problems. The program was already behind schedule when the United States prevailed upon Ukraine early in 1998 to agree not to transfer turbines for the reactor. These can be manufactured in Russia, but production facilities there will need to be retooled to do so, imposing additional costs and delays to construction.[27] Several weeks later, Russia announced that it would take over parts of the project previously run by Iran, to prevent it from falling further behind schedule.[28] The Bushehr reactor is thus not likely to be completed before the first years of the twenty-first century.

There are also disturbing signs that both China and Russia are prepared to renege on recent commitments to the United States concerning nuclear technology transfers to Iran. In October 1997, Chinese president Jiang Zemin promised President Bill Clinton that China would cease all nuclear cooperation with Iran. Yet, in January 1998, the United States reportedly obtained intelligence indicating that Iran and China had discussed the transfer of a uranium conversion plant to Iran. China subsequently quashed the deal—at least temporarily—after Washington protested to Beijing.[29] Likewise, Russia is reportedly still considering the sale to Iran of a 40-MWt (megawatt-thermal) research reactor and perhaps also a gas centrifuge enrichment facility that were part of a January 1995 nuclear cooperation accord with Iran, even though Russian president Boris Yeltsin promised Clinton during a May 1995 summit that he would not transfer this technology.[30] These transfers would significantly augment Iran's civilian nuclear infrastructure and could contribute to Iran's efforts to acquire a nuclear weapons capability.

In this regard, IRGC commander Safavi's remarks during an April 1998 meeting with IRGC naval officers have raised unsettling questions about the willingness of at least some conservative hardliners to adhere to Iran's arms control commitments. In his comments, which were subsequently leaked to the Iranian press, Safavi reportedly asked his audience: "Can we withstand America's threats and domineering attitude with a policy of détente? Can we foil dangers coming from America through dialogue between civilizations? Will we be able to protect the Islamic Republic from international Zionism by signing conventions to ban proliferation of chemical and nuclear weapons?"[31]

Safavi's disparaging comments about the NPT and the Chemical Weapons Convention (CWC) suggest that some in Iran would like to ignore the country's arms control commitments. Moreover, the fact that it was Safavi who made these comments is particularly important. The IRGC is believed to be in charge of Iran's chemical, biological, and nuclear weapons programs, as well as the country's missile forces. Safavi's opinions on these matters therefore carry great weight and are likely to have some—perhaps a decisive—impact on Iranian decision making pertaining to the CWC and NPT. In both cases, it would seem that Safavi's preference would be somehow to circumvent these treaties.

In January 1998, Iran formally joined the CWC, which requires its signatories to declare their inventories of chemical weapons within thirty days and to destroy them within ten years. Iran has not yet submitted its declaration (though many other countries—including the United States—also have not). Iran has several options:

- comply fully with the CWC by declaring and destroying its chemical arsenal, while retaining a rapid breakout capability—in the form of a surge production capacity that can be activated in a matter of days in the event of a crisis or war;

- declare and destroy its less effective agents (such as its cyanidal agents) while secretly keeping stocks of more lethal agents (such as nerve gas) and retaining a surge production capability; or

- deny possessing any chemical weapons while hiding existing inventories (probably not a credible option given Iran's use of chemical weapons during the latter phases of its war with Iraq).

It seems unlikely that Iran would give up a potentially important tactical force multiplier and the core component of its strategic deterrent while Iraq may still retain a chemical and biological warfare capability. Thus, Iran will probably pursue the second option, which ostensibly provides a way for it to meet its international commitments while addressing the concerns of those decision makers who see chemical weapons as a crucial component of Iran's defense. This option also holds out a reasonable chance of success, as experience in Iraq shows that a sophisticated effort to conceal a residual chemical weapons arsenal can succeed, even against highly intrusive inspections. It will therefore be interesting to see how Iran handles the issue of its CWC declaration, which will be a key indicator of its willingness to meet its international arms control commitments.

In the nuclear arena, Safavi's comments reinforce suspicions that Iran is using its civilian nuclear program as a stepping stone to a military program. Iran's strategy apparently is to acquire civilian nuclear technology that also has military applications, while avoiding significant activities contrary to its NPT commitments that could prematurely halt its procurement efforts and result in harsh international sanctions. In this regard, Iran has three options:

- create a civilian nuclear infrastructure capable of rapidly producing a nuclear weapon if the regional threat environment were to change;

- use its civilian program to acquire the expertise and know-how required to embark on a clandestine parallel nuclear program once all the necessary building-blocks for a military program are in place, so that a cut-off in foreign assistance in the event of discovery would not hinder these efforts; or

- create a clandestine parallel weapons program concurrent with its efforts to build up its declared civilian nuclear infrastructure.[32]

From Iran's perspective, all three options have drawbacks. In option one, the threat environment could change very quickly (if Iraq were to acquire fissile material from the former Soviet Union or if tensions in Afghanistan were to lead to a confrontation with Pakistan), and it simply is not possible to create a rapid nuclear break-out capability. Because of the nature of the technology, a decision to "go nuclear" could take months to implement. During this time, Iran would face a window of vulnerability.[33] In option two, if a clandestine Iranian nuclear weapons program were discovered, Iran would face sanctions and censure—though it would eventually get "the Bomb." In option three, if a clandestine parallel program were prematurely compromised, Iran would be censured, sanctioned, and without a nuclear weapon—the worst of all worlds, from Tehran's perspective. Yet, this option might provide the quickest route to a nuclear weapons capability.

For these reasons, Safavi and his opinions may enjoy widespread support in the regime. Moreover, Khatami and his reform-minded, liberal allies are Persian nationalists and are interested in building a strong Iran. Missiles and WMD are probably the fastest route to this goal, as Iran lacks the money to fund a major conventional military buildup. In this light, it seems plausible that Khatami and his entourage would support the acquisition of these weapons. Indeed, it should be remembered that it was Mohajerani, Khatami's liberal minister of culture and Islamic guidance, who in October 1992 called on Iran to develop nuclear weapons to counter Israel's capabilities in this area.[34] In this context, there is no contradiction between being a liberal and supporting the development of nuclear weapons. On the other hand, the fact that Safavi said what he did indicates that there may be people in Iran—perhaps in the Foreign Ministry and elsewhere—pressing for Iran to adhere to its arms control commitments. Clearly, it would be hard for a president who ran on a "rule of law" platform and who would like to reintegrate Iran into the international community to justify the violation of international commitments and treaty obligations. President Khatami might thus find it difficult to reconcile the two goals, though the matter may not be his to decide. It remains to be seen whether Safavi and like-minded individuals carry the day.

TERRORISM AND OPPOSITION TO THE PEACE PROCESS

Since President Khatami's election, several senior officials have condemned terrorism. In November 1997, Foreign Minister Kamal Kharrazi condemned a terrorist attack on tourists by Egypt's underground Islamic group; in early January 1998, Foreign Ministry spokesman Mahmoud Mohammadi condemned attacks on civilians in Algeria; and President Khatami condemned attacks on innocent civilians, including Israelis, in his January CNN message to the American people. These are all positive steps.[35]

Despite these positive public statements, Iran continues to support groups engaged in terrorism and to assassinate opponents of the clerical regime. Iran still funds, trains, and arms groups that engage in terrorism; senior Iranian officials continue meeting with representatives of terrorist groups such as Islamic Jihad, Hamas, and Hizballah (Khatami himself met with Hizballah secretary general Hassan Nasrallah in Tehran one month before Hizballah tried infiltrating a suicide bomber into Israel in November 1997); Iranian intelligence continues to stalk American personnel in Bosnia, the Persian Gulf, and Tajikistan, to gain information that would be needed for terrorist attacks on Americans (and perhaps to send a message that Iran can target American interests should it decide to do so); and Tehran continues to attack opponents of the regime.[36]

In recent years, Iran has generally restricted attacks on oppositionists to those based out of northern and central Iraq. This marks a continued evolution in Iranian policy since the early- to mid-1990s away from high profile terrorist actions in the heart of Europe (which had a harmful impact on Iranian relations with countries such as France and Germany) toward less conspicuous acts in less politically sensitive locations. It also shows that Iran is sensitive to the political costs of its involvement in terrorism and that it may be possible to alter Iranian policy in this area. Another hopeful sign is the apparent decrease in attacks on oppositionists since Khatami's election. According to one U.S. government official, of the thirteen or so assassinations that occurred in 1997, at least two occurred after Khatami's inauguration.[37] Although it is distressing that these activities continue, it is important to note this trend. One hopes that Tehran will soon move to halt its involvement in terrorism completely; this has not yet happened.

Iran continues to arm and train the Lebanese organization Hizballah, which has engaged in terrorist attacks on Jewish and Israeli targets in the past.[38] Likewise, in the past, Iranian intelligence personnel have been involved directly in terrorist attacks in Israel and on Israeli interests; Iran is not known to have been associated with any such attempts since President Khatami's election. On the other hand, Iran's continued refusal to cooperate with Argentina's investigation of the 1992 and 1994 bombings of Israeli and Jewish targets in Buenos Aires led to a deterioration in relations between the two countries in May 1998.[39] Thus, Iran's past involvement in terrorism has affected its ties with various countries and will continue to do so for years to come, even if Iran were immediately to cease its involvement in terrorism. It is worth noting, however, that some U.S. government intelligence analysts believe that Khatami and his supporters "wish to change Iranian policy with regard to terrorism . . . in a direction that would relieve some of the impediments to improved relations between Iran and western countries." According to this assessment, Khatami has been unable to do so because he does not control the relevant levers of power in Tehran.[40]

It should be mentioned, however, that in the past, different factions in the Iranian government have used a variety of means—including terrorism—to undercut the policies of their rivals. This was the background to the seizure of the American embassy in Tehran in 1979 and the leaking of U.S. efforts to create an opening with Iran in 1985–1986 (producing the Iran–Contra affair). One danger that must therefore be considered, in looking to the future, is the possibility that domestic opponents of President Khatami's policies could resort to various means—including terrorism against Americans—to embarrass and discredit Khatami and to scuttle new attempts at a political opening between the two countries.

With regard to the Arab–Israeli conflict, Iranian leaders from Khatami to Khamene'i continue to show unremitting hostility toward Israel in their public utterances, and there continues to be little difference between the different poles of the Iranian political spectrum on this subject. Yet, Iran's approach toward the Arab–Israeli peace process and the possibility of an Israeli withdrawal from Lebanon has changed somewhat since Khatami's election. In a meeting during the December

1997 Organization of the Islamic Conference (OIC) summit in Tehran, Khatami reportedly indicated to Palestine Liberation Organization leader Yasir Arafat that, although he had little faith that the Madrid process would produce a lasting Arab–Israeli peace, Iran was prepared to accept any terms that the PLO agreed to, and that it would not actively oppose or seek to undermine a peace agreement.[41] Khatami struck this general theme during his CNN interview, saying, "We have declared our opposition to the Middle East peace process [but] we do not intend to impose our views on others or to stand in their way."[42] Given the difficulties that the peace process is currently facing, however, it seems unlikely that this Iranian commitment will be tested anytime soon. More recently, Foreign Minister Kharrazi indicated that if Israel withdrew from Lebanon, "the aims of the resistance would have been achieved in reality."[43] In the past, Iranian officials would have welcomed an Israeli withdrawal as a first step on the road to the liberation of Jerusalem. In this light, Kharrazi's recent statement is worth noting, though it could also be seen as a simple statement of fact that does not speak to what would happen after an Israeli withdrawal.

CONCLUSIONS

It is difficult to judge the future direction of Iran's security and defense policies. To some degree, this will be determined by the outcome of the ongoing power struggle in Tehran between President Khatami and his hardline conservative rivals. But even if Khatami and his supporters succeed in fending off these challenges, major changes in Iranian policy in the defense arena are not likely, as Khatami does not hold the key levers of power in this area. Were Khatami free to pursue his own foreign and defense policies, it is possible that Tehran's approach to terrorism might change, though it seems unlikely that its policies toward the Arab–Israeli peace process and

Iran Under Khatami

WMD and missile proliferation would vary significantly from its current policies in these areas.

Iran's conventional procurement plans are not likely to be affected by the country's domestic power struggle. Tehran has been curtailing conventional arms procurement for financial reasons for several years now, and in light of the near- to mid-term outlook for oil prices, this trend is likely to continue for the foreseeable future, with Iran continuing to favor local production over foreign procurement.

As for terrorism, this might be the first area where a change in Iranian policy concerning the three issues of primary concern to the United States (terror, opposition to the Arab–Israeli peace process, and WMD) could become manifest. By exercising greater care in selecting the venues for and targets of terrorist attacks in recent years (i.e., focusing primarily on oppositionists based in northern and central Iraq), Iran has shown that it is sensitive to political costs. This raises the possibility that pressure could produce further change in this area. Moreover, Iran's involvement in terrorism has sullied the nation's reputation and complicated ties with many other countries. Those Iranians who want their country to abandon its involvement in terrorism should therefore be able to make a strong case for their position on the basis of the national interest. On the other hand, for hardline conservatives who support a confrontational approach to the Arabs, the United States, Israel, and expatriate oppositionists, terrorism provides a means to project Iranian influence far from the country's borders and to intimidate Iran's enemies. For these individuals, terrorism is a lever they will be loath to abandon.

Iran's opposition to Israel and the Arab–Israeli peace process serves as a form of ideological legitimation for the country's clerical leadership, even if the great majority of Iranians are largely indifferent to events in the Israeli–Palestinian arena. For this reason, it seems unlikely that Iran will abandon its harsh anti-Israel rhetoric anytime soon. Likewise, Iran is unlikely to make any further changes to its current declaratory policy toward the Arab–Israeli peace process, and it is unlikely to cease providing political and financial support for groups like Hizballah, the Palestinian Islamic Jihad, or Hamas. Moreover, efforts to press Iran to halt military assistance to groups opposed to the peace process are likely to be contingent on developments in Iran itself. Much of the economic and military aid that Iran provides to Palestinian rejectionist groups is funneled via various *bonyads* (politically well-connected charitable institutions) that are not under direct government control, but that often work in conjunction with various government ministries and enjoy the protective patronage of Supreme Leader Khamene'i. Thus, even if Khatami and his supporters desired to halt this assistance, they may not be able to do so until the bonyads are reined in, and this is unlikely to happen anytime soon, because of their political and economic clout. Moreover, given that it has been impossible to halt the flow of funds and support from wealthy individuals in moderate, pro-Western, Arab countries in the Gulf (and even the United States) to terrorist groups active in the region and beyond, it is unrealistic to expect a total halt of such support from individuals or private foundations in Iran. It is appropriate, however, for Washington to make the halt of all *official* Iranian military assistance to terrorist groups, and a good-faith effort by the Iranian government to end support by individuals and the bonyads, preconditions for a more normal relationship with the United States.

Iran's WMD and missile programs may be the most problematic issue in the long run. Iran will resist dismantling its existing capabilities or abandoning its ambitions in this area, because of its abiding concerns about threats from a resurgent Iraq, the United States, and Israel; its inability to sustain a major conventional buildup because of a lack of funds; and the fact that missiles and WMD may be the only realistic way for Iran to bridge the gap between its military weakness and its aspirations to regional power status. Moreover, Iran's efforts to acquire WMD and missiles (unlike its involvement in terrorism or its efforts to obstruct the Arab–Israeli peace process) would probably enjoy broad popular support among Iranians of all political persuasions, were this issue to be debated in the public arena. Yet, the fact that Iran is a signatory to the Biological Weapons Convention, the CWC, and the NPT makes the potential costs of cheating on its treaty obligations very high and would undermine Iran's efforts to gain recognition as a responsible member of the international community.[44] Thus, both Tehran and Washington will have to contemplate difficult tradeoffs and make politically difficult and domestically controversial decisions as they seek to establish a more normal relationship in the future.

NOTES

1. Kenneth M. Pollack, "Iran: Shaking Up the High Command," The Washington Institute for Near East Policy, *PolicyWatch* no. 269, October 1, 1997, pp. 1–2.

2. The dismissal of IRGC commander Mohsen Reza'i was considered by some a punishment for his failure to deliver the Revolutionary Guard vote for conservative presidential candidate 'Ali Akbar Nateq Nuri. The IRGC is widely believed to have voted for Khatami in the same proportions as the general population (i.e., around 69 percent).

3. Kenneth Katzman, "The Revolutionary Guard Under Khatami," unpublished paper, February 13, 1998.

4. Pollack, "Iran: Shaking Up the High Command," p. 1.

5. "Iran's Revolutionary Guards Chief Threatens to Crack Down on Liberal Dissent," Agence France Presse (AFP), April 29, 1998; "Iran Guards Chief Blasts Liberalization, Critics," Reuters, April 30, 1998. Safavi, however, appears to have misjudged the political climate in Iran. His open criticism of political leaders—including

his criticism of Khatami's call for a civilizational dialogue with America—provoked a firestorm of criticism.

6.   Khatami subsequently delivered a similar warning in August 1998 to the armed forces, urging them to stay above political factionalism. This indicates that some senior clerics are worried about the possibility that the military might intervene in the political process in one way or another. "Iran's Khatami Tells Military to Avoid Politics," Reuters, August 1, 1998.

7.   Limited evidence would likewise seem to indicate that Khatami also enjoys the support of many members of the Basij militia, which nominally falls under the control of the IRGC. For instance, in May 1998, Tehran University Basij students held a pro-Khatami rally; see "Students Hold Meeting in Tehran University," Islamic Republic News Agency (IRNA) online, May 19, 1998.

8.   Ansar-e Hezbollah is a loosely organized group of street toughs and thugs connected to hardline conservative clerics. Their patrons use them as "enforcers" to intimidate "liberal" politicians and their supporters.

9.   Just two years ago, it seemed inconceivable that the Iranian people, widely believed to be demoralized and suffering from "revolution fatigue," could effect political change through mass action. Yet, the landslide electoral victory of President Khatami in May 1997, expectations of change brought about by his election, and the unrestrained public celebrations following Iran's qualification for the World Cup soccer championship in November 1997 (in which police were unable to enforce traditional rules of Islamic modesty and decorum), have changed the political dynamics in Iran by imbuing the Iranian people with the sense that they have the potential to effect political change in their country. This has raised the possibility of a popular explosion should Khatami be threatened by his rivals.

10.   The last major naval system known to have been delivered to Iran was its third Kilo-class submarine in January 1997.

11.   Corroboration of this assessment was offered by Defense Minister 'Ali Shamkhani in a television interview in October 1997, in which he stated that one of Iran's goals was a "drastic reduction of expenditures on arms and equipment, compared to other countries in the region (by) relying on our domestic innovations. . ." See "Ira-

nian Defense Minister on Gulf Maneuvers," Islamic Republic of Iran Broadcasting (IRIB), October 16, 1997, in FBIS-NES-97-295 (Foreign Broadcast Information Service–Near East and South Asia, online), October 22, 1997.

12. See the following articles in *Jane's Defence Weekly:* Ed Blanche, "Iran Claims Production of Jet Fighter Has Begun," October 8, 1998, p. 30; "Built in Iran: The Push for Self-Sufficiency," October 15, 1997, p. 23; Ed Blanche, "Iranian Test-Firings Back 'Missile Power' Claim," October 29, 1997, p. 4; Christopher F. Foss, "Iran Unveils Two New Powerful Thunder Guns," December 10, 1997, p. 20; and Christopher F. Foss, "Iranian Armour: Revolutionary Surge in Tank Manufacturing," January 14, 1998, pp. 23–25.

13. "Naval Commanders Preview Iran's 'Victory-8' Gulf Maneuvers," IRNA, October 8, 1997, in FBIS-NES-97-281, October 8, 1997.

14. For instance, see "Defense Minister Describes Upcoming Victory-8 Exercises," IRNA, October 7, 1997, in FBIS-NES-97-280, October 7, 1997. In fact, there is little basis for these Iranian claims. The thousands of cargo vessels and oil tankers that ply the waters of the Gulf each year are a much greater source of pollution than the twenty to thirty relatively small U.S. warships normally present there. Moreover, the amount of radiation emitted by intact depleted uranium rounds is minuscule and not considered by the U.S. Department of Defense to pose an environmental or health hazard. Finally, U.S. warships in the Gulf are not armed with chemical, biological, or nuclear weapons. The United States destroyed all its biological weapons between 1969 and 1972 and is currently in the process of destroying its remaining chemical weapons, which are located in the continental United States. The United States withdrew tactical nuclear weapons deployed on surface ships sometime after the dissolution of the Soviet Union in 1991.

15. "Khatami Visit to Kingdom to Crown Saudi–Iranian 'Honeymoon,'" *MidEast Mirror*, March 16, 1998; Caroline Faraj and Philip Finnegan "Kuwait, Iran to Hold Joint Naval Excercise," *Defense News*, February 9–15, 1998, p. 40. It should be noted, however, that this was not the first time an Iranian naval vessel had paid a port call on an Arab Gulf state. On several occasions in recent years, naval vessels from Iran and Oman have conducted reciprocal port visits.

16. "Iranian Defense Minister on Gulf Maneuvers," FBIS-NES-97-295.

17. For more on the Iraqi oil smuggling operation, see Mark Dennis, "Saddam's Nightmare," *Newsweek*, March 16, 1998, pp. 40–41; CNN, May 6, 1998.

18. It should be noted that some press reports have implied that the Iranian "diplomats" may have been military or intelligence personnel involved in supplying arms to Iran's Afghan allies. Douglas Jehl, "Iran Angered by Promise that Proved to Be Hollow," *New York Times*, September 13, 1998, p. A15. For details concerning the buildup, which reportedly included tens of thousands of troops, twenty-five strike aircraft, eighty T-72 tanks, two SA-6 surface-to-air missile batteries, ninety heavy artillery pieces, and sixty armored vehicles, see Dana Priest, "Iran Poises its Forces on Afghan Border," *Washington Post*, September 5, 1998, pp. A1, A22.

19. Douglas Jehl, "Iran's Top Leader Weighs in Against Afghans," *New York Times*, September 16, 1998, p. A10.

20. Russian Foreign Intelligence Service (FIS), *A New Challenge After the Cold War: Proliferation of Weapons of Mass Destruction* (Moscow: FIS, 1993), in Joint Publication Research Service, *Nuclear Proliferation Report* (JPRS-TND), March 5, 1993, p. 29.

21. U.S. Department of Defense, *Proliferation: Threat and Response 1997* (Washington, D.C.: Office of the Secretary, Department of Defense, 1997).

22. Michael Eisenstadt and Azriel Lorber, "Iran's Recent Missile Test: Assessment and Implications," The Washington Institute for Near East Policy, *PolicyWatch* no. 330, August 5, 1998, p. 1.

23. Robin Wright, "Russia Warned on Helping Iran Missile Program," *Los Angeles Times*, February 12, 1997, pp. A1, A6; Bill Gertz, "Russia, China Aid Iran's Missile Program," *Washington Times*, September 10, 1997, p. A1; Barton Gellman, "Shift by Iran Fuels Debate Over Sanctions," *Washington Post*, December 31, 1997, p. A1; Thomas W. Lippman, "U.S. Keeps After Russia to Halt Flow of Missile Technology to Iran," *Washington Post*, January 18, 1998, p. A9; David A. Fulghum, "Slipup Spoils Coverage of Iranian Missile Test," *Aviation Week & Space Technology*, August 3, 1998, pp. 24–25.

24. Barbara Opall, "U.S. Queries China on Iran," *Defense News*, June 19–25, 1995, p. 1; Bill Gertz, "Russia Disregards Pledge to Curb Iran Missile Output," *Washington Times*, May 22, 1997, p. A3; Bill Gertz, "China Joins Forces with Iran on Short-Range Missile," *Washington Times*, June 17, 1997, p. A3; Gertz, "Russia, China Aid Iran's Missile Program."

25. Michael Eisenstadt, *Iranian Military Power: Capabilities and Intentions* (Washington, D.C.: The Washington Institute for Near East Policy, 1996), pp. 9–25.

26. "Iran Says Need to Build More Nuclear Plants," Reuters, October 3, 1997.

27. David B. Ottaway and Dan Morgan, "U.S., Ukraine at Odds Over Nuclear Technology Transfer," *Washington Post*, February 8, 1998, p. A25; Michael R. Gordon, "Russia Plans to Sell Reactors to Iran Despite U.S. Protests," *New York Times*, March 7, 1998, p. A3.

28. David Hoffman, "Russia Expanding Role in Iranian Power Plant," *Washington Post*, February 22, 1998, p. A30.

29. Barton Gellman, "U.S. Action Stymied China Sale to Iran," *Washington Post*, March 13, 1998, p. A1; Bill Gertz, "China in New Nuclear Sales Effort," *Washington Times*, March 13, 1998, p. A1. It is particularly disturbing that one or two years prior to this incident, China had promised the United States that it would cancel the conversion plant deal.

30. David Makovsky, "Iran Negotiating with Russia for a Reactor," *Ha'aretz Internet Edition*, February 18, 1998; Bill Gertz, "Russian Arms Deals with Iran Worry U.S.," *Washington Times*, May 7, 1998, p. A1.

31. "Iran's Revolutionary Guards Chief Threatens to Crack Down on Liberal Dissent," AFP, April 29, 1998; "Iran Guards Chief Blasts Liberalization, Critics," Reuters, April 30, 1998.

32. In the first and second options, Iran could engage in nuclear weapons–related research and development under the cover of a defensive program ostensibly intended to provide an understanding of the nature of the nuclear threat posed by Iraq, Israel, and the United States (in much the same way that Sweden concealed its investigation of a nuclear option in the late 1950s and early 1960s in its own

"defensive program"). Thus, Iran could make progress in the weapons design area without unambiguously violating its NPT commitments, and probably with a very low likelihood of getting caught. For more on the Swedish "defensive program," see Paul M. Cole, "Atomic Bombast: Nuclear Weapon Decision-Making in Sweden, 1946-72," *The Washington Quarterly* (Spring 1997), pp. 233–251.

33. This is clearly the lesson Iraq learned during the 1991 Gulf War. After its August 1990 invasion of Kuwait, Iraq initiated a crash program to produce one or two nuclear weapons within about eight months, using diverted reactor fuel. The outbreak of the Gulf War in January 1991 preempted these plans, which were running behind schedule anyway. This experience underscored the importance of possessing a "nuclear force in being." Possessing a latent nuclear weapon production capability, or a "virtual nuclear arsenal" may not, in some circumstances, provide a hedge against disaster.

34. Steve Coll, "Tehran Ambiguous on its A-Arms Plans," *Washington Post*, November 17, 1992, p. A30.

35. See the Department of State's annual report, *Patterns of Global Terrorism 1997,* on the internet at <http://www.state.gov/www/global/terrorism/1997Report/1997index.html>. In his CNN interview, Khatami stated that "any form of killing of innocent men and women who are not involved in confrontations is terrorism" and that "terrorism should be condemned in all its forms"; CNN, January 7, 1998, on the internet at <http://cnn.com/WORLD/9801/07/iran/interview.html>.

36. Bill Gertz, "Intelligence Agency Highlights Threat of Anti-American Terror in Tajikistan," *Washington Times*, December 9, 1997, p. A6; Hillary Mann, "Iranian Links to International Terrorism—The Khatami Era," The Washington Institute for Near East Policy, *PolicyWatch* no. 269, January 28, 1998. IRGC chief Safavi implied that Tehran was capable of conducting terrorism on a global basis when he declared in an September 1997 speech that the IRGC and its Basij militia were prepared to respond to foreign aggression by retaliating not just in the Persian Gulf region, but around the world. "IRGC Head: Iran Ready to Meet Aggressors; Be Security Force," IRNA, September 19, 1997, in FBIS-NES-97-262, September 19, 1997.

37. Testimony of Martin Indyk, assistant secretary of state for Near Eastern affairs, before the Senate Foreign Relations Committee, Subcommittee on Near East and South Asian Affairs, May 14, 1998. Although the number of assassinations that occurred following Khatami's inauguration constituted a dramatic reduction over the number that occurred during the first half of the year, the tempo of such operations since Khatami came to power is more or less the same as the previous five years (in which Iran consistently averaged about half a dozen assassinations a year).

38. This most recent terrorism attempt involved a German convert to Islam, Stefan Josef Smyrek, who had undergone military training with Hizballah in Lebanon. "Israel Fears New Hezbollah Attacks," *Washington Times*, December 26, 1997, p. A13.

39. The cultural attaché at Iran's embassy in Buenos Aires—who was also the prayer leader of a local mosque—is believed to have played a central role in the bombing of the Jewish Community Center in 1994. He was declared persona non grata after leaving Argentina in 1997. Clifford Krauss, "Argentina Arrests 8 and Ousts 7 in Anti-Jewish Bombings," *New York Times,* May 17, 1998, p. A15.

40. R. Jeffrey Smith, "Terrorism, Officials Say," *Washington Post*, May 5, 1998, p. A9.

41. Robin Wright, "Clinton Encourages More Exchanges, Better Ties with Iran, *Los Angeles Times*, January 30, 1998, p. A6.

42. See the transcript of Khatami's CNN interview at <http://cnn.com/WORLD/9801/07/iran/interview.html>. It should be noted, however, that former President 'Ali Akbar Hashemi Rafsanjani made a similar promise in 1994, saying that "we do not wish to intervene in practice and physically disrupt the [Arab–Israeli peace] process," even as Iran was providing political, economic, and military support to Lebanese and Palestinian groups opposed to the peace process. "Rafsanjani: Iran Will Not Act to Disrupt the Peace Process," *MidEast Mirror*, June 8, 1994, p. 15.

43. "Iran Says No U.S. Plan for Diplomat in Tehran," Reuters, March 30, 1998.

44. Iran's missile programs do not violate any treaty prohibition, and for this reason Iran is likely to continue with them for the foreseeable future.

Chapter 5

OPPORTUNITIES AND CHALLENGES FOR U.S. POLICY

Patrick Clawson and Michael Eisenstadt

The May 1997 election of Iranian president Muhammad Khatami poses both opportunities and challenges for U.S. policy toward the Islamic Republic. On the one hand, it holds out, for the first time since the 1979 revolution, the prospect of more normal relations with the Tehran. It also provides an opportunity for the United States to test the willingness of the new Iranian government to alter its policies in the areas of greatest concern to the United States: terrorism, violent opposition to the Arab–Israeli peace process, and the development of weapons of mass destruction (WMD) and the missiles to deliver them.

Clearly, U.S. policy needs to respond to recent developments in Tehran. But how? In the past, U.S. policy relied largely on pressure to achieve its objectives vis-à-vis Iran. Now, a mix of pressures and incentives are needed. But what kind of mix is most likely to lead to an outcome favorable to U.S. interests? Furthermore, what role should President Khatami play in U.S. calculations? Should the United States be working to bolster his position vis-à-vis his adversaries, or should it be more concerned with engaging and encouraging those who brought him to power—the Iranian people? Finally, how does the United States enhance the possibility of government-to-government talks—which Khatami has rejected for now—but which is the only viable framework for dealing with and resolving the difficult issues dividing Iran and the United

States? And in the absence of official contacts, what can the United States do to advance its interests?

U.S. POLICY TOWARD IRAN: AN ASSESSMENT

Although sometimes portrayed as a failure, U.S. policy toward Iran since the 1979 revolution can in fact claim a number of important achievements.

First, Washington has had some success in curbing Tehran's ability to threaten U.S. allies and interests by denying Iran access to arms and technology and the hard currency necessary to fund such arms and technology transfers. U.S. pressure, diplomatic demarches, and interdiction operations have thwarted several major conventional arms deals and countless smaller ones;[1] cut Iran off from Western arms and technology sources—forcing it to rely on less advanced suppliers such as North Korea, China, and Russia; and hindered procurement of spare parts for its armed forces, thereby making it more difficult for Tehran to maintain its existing force structure. This has made Iran careful to avoid a confrontation with the United States that could lead to losses it knows it could neither absorb nor afford to replace.

U.S. sanctions have made an important contribution to U.S. security by depriving Iran of the resources it could otherwise have used for a military buildup. Iran's economic woes—which have been exacerbated by U.S. sanctions—have forced Tehran to cut military procurement since 1989 by more than half and delayed its efforts to acquire conventional arms and WMD. Thus, following the Iran–Iraq War, Iran's Majlis (parliament) announced plans to spend $2 billion a year for five years for weapons purchases. Actual spending, however, has fallen far short of this target.[2] Accordingly, in the period 1989–1996, the actual numbers of weapons Iran has obtained also fell far short, in most categories, of its acquisition goals. Thus, while Tehran had been hoping to obtain some 1,000–1,500 tanks, it acquired about 225; of 250–500 infantry fighting vehicles, it acquired about 80; and of 100–200 aircraft, it acquired about 65. The only areas in which Iranian procurement objectives may have been met were in the area of field artillery and warships; Iran acquired 320 artillery pieces and thirteen warships.[3] The reason for the overall shortfall, however, was a lack of money, in large part because of low oil prices and, starting in 1993, U.S. pressure against loans to Iran.[4]

Lacking the funds to sustain a major, across-the-board military buildup, Iran has had to content itself with selectively enhancing its military capabilities. Moreover, that shortfall in Iranian arms spending has had a significant impact on the balance of power in the Persian Gulf. With an extra $1 billion to $2 billion a year, Iran would have been able to add many more weapons, complicating U.S. defense planning in the region.

Second, U.S. sanctions have exacerbated Iran's deep-seated economic problems, which have been an important factor in generating popular dissatisfaction with clerical rule. Without U.S. technology and without funding from international capital markets, Iran will be hard pressed to increase oil output—which still generates 80 percent of all foreign exchange earnings. Moreover, oil income will be stagnant, whereas the population is increasing rapidly. The children of the postrevolution baby boom, which conservative mullahs had encouraged, are now graduating high school and looking for work. Iran has been able to create only 350,000 jobs annually for the 800,000 young men joining the labor force each year (not to mention Iran's young women). Iran thus badly needs the foreign capital that U.S. containment impedes. Washington's ability to help Iran mitigate its financial problems by easing or lifting sanctions provides a great deal of leverage over Tehran.

Many Iranians realize that the country's economic prospects are poor unless it can raise large amounts of foreign capital, and that the only way to do so is to improve relations with the West—in particular, the United States. That has been an element in the support for President Khatami, who has repeatedly stated his desire to improve relations with the West. Whereas sanctions-induced economic pain probably was a rather small factor in Khatami's election—domestic issues predominated in that contest, as in most elections in most countries—U.S. sanctions have probably had the unintended but welcome effect of encouraging the evolution of Iranian politics in a direction that serves U.S. interests.

Sanctions have hurt Iran, as many Iranians now acknowledge. Their impact has been magnified by Iran's inappropriate economic policies, a relatively large foreign debt obligation dating to the early 1990s, and the rapid decline in world oil prices starting in late 1997. Because of the drop in oil prices, Iran's net oil exports in 1998 may be only $10 billion, compared to $16 billion in 1996. Suffering from economic distress caused by low oil prices, heavy debt-service obligations, and heightened expectations of socioeconomic change, Iran is particularly vulnerable to continued U.S. economic pressure. Thus, the United States is in a strong bargaining position vis-à-vis Iran; it should play its hand accordingly. Sanctions should be eased or lifted only in return for major concessions by Iran—not as a goodwill or confidence-building measure. And if Tehran refuses to alter its policy in areas of concern to the United States, at the very least sanctions will compel Iran to continue spending more on butter than on guns in the coming years, thereby slowing Iran's military expansion and modernization efforts and constraining Tehran's ability to threaten U.S. allies or interests in the region, should President Khatami's hardline conservative rivals assume a more assertive role in the foreign policy arena.

How, then, to assess U.S. policy? Whereas neither the United States nor Europe can claim success regarding efforts to alter Iranian policy, U.S. efforts to deny Iran arms, technology, and income through sanctions and other means have imposed opportunity costs on Iran, whose economy would be more productive and whose military would be more intimidating and powerful without such restrictions. And U.S. diplomatic efforts have reduced Iran's access to dual-use technology needed for WMD production and have reduced the freedom with which Iranian intelligence agents operate in Western countries. On the down side, U.S. pressure on allies to halt loans to Iran and secondary sanctions passed in 1996 (the Iran–Libya Sanctions Act, or ILSA) have raised tensions with key U.S. allies in Europe. The challenge is how to maintain pressure on Tehran in response to its pursuit of policies inimical to U.S. interests in the Middle East, while reducing tensions with Europe over the frictions that arise from Europe and America's divergent approaches toward Iran.

THE NEED TO 'HANG TOUGH'

President Khatami's election and his opening to the American people have significantly altered the rules of the game and greatly complicated Washington's calculations in a way that will require the United States to modify its approach toward Iran. If it is to avoid the dangers and grasp the opportunities created by these new circumstances, Washington will need to muster a degree of sophistication, restraint, and subtlety that has been largely lacking in U.S. policy toward Iran until now. The United States can no longer rely exclusively on a policy based on sanctions.

The U.S. reaction to Khatami's election has reflected a recognition of this fact. Washington's initial response was cautious but hopeful. This is understandable in light of the history of the U.S.–Iran relationship. Two presidents (Jimmy Carter and Ronald Reagan) have been "burned" in their dealings with Iran, and it is understandable that President Bill Clinton and his administration would move slowly and cautiously in seeking to respond to the opening created by Khatami's election. Moreover, America's initial responses—welcoming Khatami's election; placing the oppositionist Mojahedin-e Khalq on a terrorist watch list as a gesture to Tehran; encouraging wrestling and soccer diplomacy and other forms of people-to-people contacts; easing visa restrictions on Iranian tourists, travel restrictions on United Nations—based Iranian diplomats, and travel warnings for Americans wanting to visit Iran; and offering a roadmap for improved relations—were all well-considered steps. Yet, more could and should be done.

If U.S. policy is to be faulted, it should be—paradoxically—for being both insufficiently resolute in maintaining tough sanctions that have borne beneficial results in the past, and yet neither imaginative nor daring enough in responding to changed circumstances in Tehran.

Events in early 1998 give reason to believe that the United States is retreating from its successful sanctions policy, largely for reasons unrelated to developments in Iran. Facing a conflict with European Union (EU) members over the U.S. secondary boycott of firms that invest in Iran's oil and gas industry—a boycott mandated by ILSA—the Clinton administration decided to grant a waiver for the first investment that would have triggered the law: a $2 billion project to develop the South Pars gas and oil field by the French firm Total in association with the Russian firm Gazprom and the Malaysian firm Petronas. Other less important factors contributing to the decision to back off from the secondary boycott were the U.S. business community's lobbying against sanctions of all kinds—which undercut Congress's willingness to take a strong stand regarding sanctions on Iran—and the desire to make some sort of gesture to President Khatami.

The Clinton administration misplayed its hand in the South Pars deal, which was a poor case for the United States to oppose—Total sold most of its U.S. assets three days before announcing the deal, and the French government stood to gain on the domestic political scene by standing up to U.S. pressure. ILSA was crafted to provide great flexibility for such cases, but the Clinton administration did not exploit the opportunities available to it. For instance, the U.S. government could have quickly placed limited sanctions on Total. The law requires choosing two of six specific measures, and two of them—denial of credits from the Export–Import Bank and refusal of permission to be a primary dealer in U.S. government securities—are entirely outside the domain of the World Trade Organization (WTO). Had Washington applied such sanctions against Total, France would have had no basis for a WTO complaint, and Washington could have sustained the deterrent effect of ILSA by hinting darkly that it would react more severely against firms more vulnerable than Total.

It could be argued that a general waiver of ILSA was and is in the U.S. interest, because the strong EU reaction has shown that ILSA does not work or that its cost is too high. The Clinton administration approach—a project-specific waiver for the South Pars deal plus strong hints that similar waivers would be granted for any other EU investment, except investment in a pipeline crossing Iran from Caspian states—goes much of the way toward defusing the tension with Europe. Yet, it undermines the deterrent value of ILSA, in that it looks like a general waiver, even though the EU has not fulfilled the principle criterion set out in the legislation before a general waiver can be given: the application of economic pressure against Iran.

The time to have decided if a general waiver was appropriate and to announce the waiver would have been just after Khatami's inaugural in August 1997, the month before the South Pars deal was announced. Had that been done, the waiver could have been presented as a U.S. olive branch to the new government, which would have put the ball in Iran's court to respond. By waiting instead until May 1998 to waive ILSA for the South Pars deal, the Clinton administration gave the impression that it will not follow-up its strong declaratory policy with tough actions. This could raise questions about American resolve and invite further challenges to U.S. policies.

A separate track has been the imposition of sanctions on firms providing Iran with WMD and missile technology. Russia and China have repeatedly demonstrated a disturbing tendency to violate commitments made to the United States by transferring sensitive arms and technology to Iran when they believe they can get away with it. The United States has imposed sanctions on Chinese companies accused of transferring chemical weapons precursors and on Russian companies accused of transferring ballistic missile–related technologies to Iran. (In the latter case, sanctions were imposed in accordance with a Presidential Executive Order, and not in accordance with the Iran Missile Proliferation Sanctions Act, which Congress passed overwhelmingly but President Clinton vetoed.) Whereas a vigorous debate about the role of sanctions legislation is likely to continue, sanctions punishing Russian and Chinese companies that engage in WMD and missile technology transfers are likely to remain a core component of U.S. policy toward Iran for the foreseeable future. Moreover, experience has shown that comprehensive sanctions that deny Tehran hard currency have helped to slow Iranian military procurement, and for this reason such sanctions are likely to remain a cornerstone of U.S. policy as well.

SANCTIONS AND DIALOGUE CAN GO HAND-IN-HAND

Sanctions are part of a policy to pressure Iran, not to isolate it. Indeed, U.S. interests are well served by more contact with Iranians at all levels. An important initiative in this domain is the Radio Free Iran broadcasts to Iran, which can crack the monopoly of electronic news there. Radio Free Iran will show Iranians that the United States supports the sort of relatively pluralistic free debate already present in Iran's low-circulation print press, which strongly contrasts with the strictly controlled and viciously anti-Western radio and television stations.

The long-standing U.S. position is that it is open to a dialogue with official Iranian government representatives, though not with self-styled intermediaries. Although the United States might not have been eager for such an official dialogue in times past, Washington would certainly be interested in talking with the Khatami government. Khatami has shown some signs that he may modify Iran's stance both toward Washington and on issues of importance to the United States. Moreover, although Khatami has repeatedly rejected official dialogue with the United States, technical meetings of various sorts—attended by both U.S. and Iranian representatives—have become more common.

There is no contradiction between holding an official dialogue with and continuing sanctions on Tehran. Dialogue and sanctions can go hand in hand; the United States followed such a policy toward the Soviet Union for decades. At the same time, the United States should be prepared to ease or lift sanctions if Iran demonstrates that it has altered or abandoned the policies that led Washington to impose sanctions in the first place. For instance, if Iran were prepared to abandon its nuclear power program—a program that provides Iran the opportunity to advance its nuclear weapons ambitions—the United States could lift its objections to World Bank lending for Iran's electricity-generating needs and could encourage Japan to restart disbursement of its blocked ¥121-billion loan for a hydroelectric dam. In fact, the United States might even be willing to organize an international consortium to develop Iran's nonnuclear power sector, if Iran were to abandon its civilian nuclear power program.

More immediate than the question of government-to-government dialogue is the issue of how to respond to the current vigorous factional struggle in Iran. Some suggest that the United States needs to find a way to support Khatami. That miscasts the issue. The United States needs to find a way to support the 20 million Iranians who voted for change, rather than to support one faction of the regime against another. Bitter experience has shown that such efforts to support one faction ("moderates") against another ("radicals") are apt to backfire, burning the United States and possibly its Iranian protégés. This was precisely the context of the seizure of the U.S. embassy in Tehran in November 1979 by radicals opposed to efforts to normalize ties with the United States. The embassy seizure also led to the forced resignation of moderate Prime Minister Mehdi Bazargan and Foreign Minister Ibrahim Yazdi and their replacement by more radical figures. It was likewise the case when, in November 1986, Iranian opponents of a political opening between Washington and Tehran leaked information to a Lebanese newspaper about American efforts to swap arms for hostages—thus creating the Iran–Contra affair.

Meanwhile, the United States needs to demonstrate that sanctions will not be eased or lifted until Iranian policy changes. Were the U.S. government to reward Iran for merely holding government-to-government talks, Iran might conclude that talk is all it needs to do. At the same time, the United States might consider some modifications of the sanctions policy. For instance, it could lift the ban on U.S. exports of consumer goods; U.S. interests are served when Iran uses its scarce foreign exchange for consumer goods rather than weapons, and U.S. firms and Iranian consumers would both benefit from the sales.

A MORE FRIENDLY APPROACH TOWARD IRANIANS

In formulating its policy toward Iran, the United States also needs to consider how its actions affect its standing in the eyes of the Iranian people, as well as its relations with Gulf Arabs and its Western European allies.

Most Iranians like Americans and admire the United States for its principles. This reservoir of goodwill is a precious asset that America must not squander. Moreover, because the Iranian people are the main engine for political change in that country, they are a source of leverage over the Iranian government. The potential offered by this leverage was most clearly manifested by President Khatami's CNN address to the American people—more than anything else a concession to popular opinion in Iran, which strongly favors normalizing relations with the United States. The interview also signified a recognition that if Tehran is to improve the economic lot of the Iranian people, it can do so only if the United States agrees to ease or lift sanctions and to cease efforts to block loans to and investments in Iran.

Moreover, there is reason to believe that the recent Saudi–Iranian rapprochement was motivated in large part by a Saudi desire to distance itself from the United States following the Khobar Towers bombing—to avoid being caught in the middle of an Iranian–U.S. clash. Efforts to reduce tensions with Tehran would reassure some of America's Gulf allies that Washington is in fact *not* headed toward confrontation with Tehran. Ongoing efforts to contain Iran will be much stronger if they enjoy the continued cooperation of America's allies in the Gulf.

Finally, demonstrating a willingness to increase contacts with Iranians and a readiness to reestablish official contacts with Tehran would strengthen America's case with its European allies. It would demonstrate that U.S. policy toward Iran is *not* driven by domestic politics, and that the United States is eager to test Iranian intentions. This would better enable the United States to make the case to its European allies that dialogue and pressure can go hand-in-hand.

Moreover, it would be a severe setback for U.S. policy if the Iranian government could make a credible case to its people and to America's allies in the Gulf and in Western Europe that the United States has spurned President Khatami's call for a dialogue between peoples, among other Iranian gestures. Tangible steps by Washington to relax tensions with Tehran would thus help the United States to test Iranian intentions, to maintain the momentum of such efforts, and, just as important, to avoid eroding its standing with both Iranians and key allies. Also, through its actions, the United States must make it clear to the Iranian people that it is *their* government that is the main obstacle to increased contact and better relations between the two countries. This could lead to additional pressure for change in Tehran.

What does this mean in terms of specific policy recommendations? Washington has taken a number of good first steps, but more can and must be done to reduce tensions with Tehran, to maintain the momentum of ongoing efforts for a rapprochement, and to signal its support for the Iranian people. Among them, Washington should

- further streamline visa application procedures to reduce obstacles for Iranians who want to visit the United States, while placing stringent limitations on those applicants who pose the greatest security concerns;

- propose stationing consular officials in Tehran to facilitate Iranian visits, though this proposal would almost certainly be unacceptable to the Iranian government at this stage;

- remove Iran from the list of major illicit-drug-producing or -transit countries in recognition of Iran's efforts in this area;

- lift the ban on exports of U.S.-made consumer goods to Iran;

- support the new Persian language service of Radio Free Iran, so the great majority of Iranians who depend on the electronic media for their information can receive the same kind of free debate that characterizes the low-circulation Tehran press;

- support efforts to intensify people-to-people contacts involving—among others—artists, agricultural and medical specialists, and American nongovernmental policy analysts who are broadly supportive of U.S. policy in the region;

- consider an extended television address by President Clinton to the Iranian people along the lines of Khatami's January CNN interview; and

- offer incentives for Iran to abandon its nuclear power program by offering to help finance and build additional non-nuclear power plants.

In short, the United States should be bold about reaching out to Iranians while maintaining pressure on Tehran—easing or lifting sanctions only in return for tangible concessions by Iran.

CONCLUSIONS

The election of President Khatami has raised hopes for the emergence of an Iran that eschews the use of terrorism as a policy instrument, observes its arms control obligations, and lives in peace with its neighbors—thereby laying the foundation for more normal relations with the United States. Such a development would help reduce regional tensions and might enable both sides to work together to contain Iraq and to use Iran as an overland route for the export of Central Asian oil.

In expressing genuine interest in the possibility of a rapprochement and endorsing President Khatami's call for people-to-people contacts, U.S. policy toward Iran has turned a corner. The major issues dividing the two countries, however, will be resolved only in the context of government-to-government talks, which Tehran has ruled out for now. The question, then, is how to move forward in the absence of such contacts. This will depend in part on developments in Tehran that are largely beyond American control. Nonetheless, there are a number of things the United States could do in the meanwhile:

- Seek out more official contacts, for instance, in the context of multilateral talks (such as at the United Nations contact group for Afghanistan), discussions about the business of international organizations, and informal discussions between U.S. and Iranian government officials during conferences of private organizations.

- Encourage people-to-people contacts to help create a psychological climate—in both countries—in which open, routine official contacts can eventually occur. This means encouraging Iran to accept more visits by American experts, scholars, and analysts, to match the number of Iranians who visit the United States. (In 1997, 21,000 Iranians visited America, whereas fewer than 1,000 Americans were allowed to visit Iran on a U.S. passport.)

- Barring major changes in Iranian foreign and defense policy, the United States should continue with efforts to delay and obstruct Tehran's efforts to modernize and expand its armed forces—particularly in the WMD and missile arena.

Efforts to delay the development of Iran's military potential are important on several levels. First, they are a hedge against the possibility of a reversion by Iran to a more aggressive foreign and defense policy in the future. Second, if and when Iran and the United States finally hold official talks, it might be easier for Tehran to trade away capabilities under development than to abandon capabilities that already exist, in return for the easing or lifting of sanctions by Washington. Third, it buys time for the United States and its allies develop countermeasures to Iranian capabilities. For instance, in 1993–1994, U.S.-orchestrated multilateral pressure on Pyongyang discouraged North Korea from transferring the Nodong-1 to Iran, forcing Tehran instead to take the more roundabout route of building a missile using North Korean–supplied production technology. That five-year delay provided the time for Israel to develop its U.S.-funded Arrow antimissile system. The first Israeli missile battery will be deployed in 1999, before the Iranian Shehab-3 is likely to become operational. Further delays in the Iranian program might likewise provide the United States with enough time to improve its own theater missile defense capabilities. Finally, assuming that the trend toward moderation and pragmatism in Iranian politics continues, it could postpone Iran's development of medium-range missiles and nuclear weapons until the time when the more moderate political elements are more firmly ensconced in Tehran. In this way, the potentially destabilizing impact of Iranian proliferation might be mitigated.

NOTES

1. In October 1997, for example, the United States purchased twenty-one MiG-29 fighters from Moldova to prevent their purchase by Iran. Bradley Graham, "U.S. Captures MiG Jets in Secret Deal," *Washington Post*, November 5, 1997, p. A23; Steven Lee Myers, "U.S. Is Buying MiGs so Rogue Nations Will Not Get Them," *New York Times*, November 5, 1997, p. A1.

2. Accurate, reliable figures on Iranian military spending is very hard to find. For instance, according to Iran Central Bank figures, actual spending on arms imports reached $1.625 billion in 1989–1990; $1.6 billion in 1990–1991; $1.678 billion in 1991–1992; $808 million in 1992–1993; and $850 million in 1993–1994 (International Monetary Fund, *Islamic Republic of Iran—Recent Economic*

Developments, September 19, 1995, p. 74, and October 5, 1993, p. 38). These figures are roughly consistent with U.S. government estimates that Iranian foreign exchange expenditures on arms dropped from a high of $2 billion in 1991 to less than $1 billion in 1997 (Bruce Riedel, "U.S. Policy in the Gulf: Five Years of Dual Containment," The Washington Institute for Near East Policy, *PolicyWatch* no. 315, May 8, 1998, p. 2).

3. Figures for arms transfers are derived from the United Nations Register of Conventional Arms, 1992 through 1996; *The Military Balance* (London: International Institute for Strategic Studies, 1992 through 1997); and *Middle East Military Balance* (Tel Aviv: Jaffee Center for Strategic Studies, 1992–1993 through 1994–1995).

4. Chinese officials relate privately that the reason China agreed to stop deliveries of advanced antiship missiles to Iran (in accordance with repeated U.S. requests) was that Tehran was behind in payments for missiles and missile boats by nearly $1 billion. In this case, economic pressure on Tehran was a more effective way to staunch Chinese missile sales to Iran than offering inducements to Iran's Chinese suppliers (such as increased access to U.S. civilian nuclear technology).